READ THIS!

Fascinating Stories from the Content Areas

Intro

Daphne Mackey

With
Wendy Asplin
Laurie Blass
Deborah Gordon
Mary March

CAMBRIDGE UNIVERSITY PRESS
Cambridge, New York, Melbourne, Madrid, Cape Town,
Singapore, São Paulo, Delhi, Tokyo, Mexico City

Cambridge University Press
32 Avenue of the Americas, New York, NY 10013-2473, USA

www.cambridge.org
Information on this title: www.cambridge.org/9781107630710

First published 2012

Printed in Hong Kong, by Golden Cup Printing Company Limited

A catalog record for this publication is available from the British Library.

Library of Congress Cataloging in Publication Data

Mackey, Daphne.
  Read this! intro : fascinating stories from the content areas / Daphne Mackey ; with Wendy Asplin ... [et al.].
    p. cm. — (Read this!)
  ISBN 978-1-107-63071-0 (pbk.)
  1. English language—Textbooks for foreign speakers. 2. Interdisciplinary approach in education.
  3. Reading comprehension. I. Title.

  PE1128.M3243 2012
  428.6'4—dc23

2011041590

ISBN 978-1-107-63071-0 Student's Book
ISBN 978-1-107-64923-1 Teacher's Manual

Book design: Adventure House, NYC
Layout services: Page Designs International
Photo research: Elizabeth Blomster
Audio production: John Marshall Media

Contents

Introduction

ABOUT THE SERIES

Read This! is a four-level reading series for beginning, low intermediate, and intermediate-level English learners. The series is designed to enhance students' confidence and enjoyment of reading in English, build their reading skills, and develop their vocabulary.

The readings in the series are high interest and content-rich. They are all nonfiction and contain fascinating true information. The style of writing makes the information easily digestible, and the language is carefully controlled at each level to make the texts just challenging enough, but easily accessible.

Each book in *Read This!* consists of five thematically related units. Each unit is loosely connected to a different academic discipline that might be studied in an institution of higher education, such as business, engineering, psychology, health care, or mathematics. Each unit is divided into three chapters, and each chapter contains a reading accompanied by exercise material. Besides the main theme of the unit, each chapter is tied to a secondary academic content area so that students can experience an interdisciplinary approach to a topic.

Accompanying each reading is a variety of pre- and postreading activities. They are designed to provide a balance of reading comprehension, vocabulary, and reading skill development. Many activities also provide opportunities for student discussion and a chance for students to connect the topics of the readings to their own lives and experience. Each unit ends with a wrap-up that reviews ideas and vocabulary from all three chapters of the unit.

Vocabulary instruction is an important focus of *Read This!* Selected words from each reading are previewed, presented, practiced, and recycled. These words are drawn from the two academic disciplines that are brought together in each reading. In addition, selected words from the Academic Word List (AWL) are pulled out from each reading for instruction.

Each unit is designed to take 6–9 hours of class time, depending on how much out-of-class work is assigned by the teacher. The units can either be taught in the order they appear or out of sequence. It is also possible to teach the chapters within a unit out of order. However, by teaching the units and chapters in sequence, students will benefit fully from the presentation, practice, and recycling of the target vocabulary.

All the readings in the *Read This!* series have been recorded for those students whose language learning can be enhanced by listening to a text as well as by reading it. However, since the goal of the series is to build students' readings skills, students should be told to read and study the texts without audio before they choose to listen to them.

The audio files can be found on the *Read This!* Web site at www.cambridge.org/readthis. Students can go to this site and listen to the audio recordings on their computers, or they can download the audio recordings onto their personal MP3 players to listen to them at any time.

An audio CD of the readings is also available in the back of each Teacher's Manual for those teachers who would like to bring the recorded readings into their classroom for students to hear. Also in the Teacher's Manual are photocopiable unit tests.

THE UNIT STRUCTURE

Unit Opener

The title, at the top of the first page of each unit, names the academic content area that unifies the three chapters in the unit. The title of each chapter also appears, along with a picture and a short blurb that hints at the content of the chapter reading. These elements are meant to intrigue readers and whet their appetites for what is to come. At the bottom of the page, the main academic content area of the unit is repeated, and the secondary academic content area for each chapter is given as well.

1 Topic Preview

The opening page of each chapter includes a picture and two tasks: Part A and Part B. Part A is usually a problem-solving task in which students are asked to bring some of their background knowledge or personal opinions to bear. Part B always consists of three discussion questions that draw students closer and closer to an idea of what the reading is about. In fact, the last question, *What do you think the reading will be about?* is always the same in every chapter: This is to help learners get into the habit of predicting what texts will be about before they read.

2 Vocabulary Preview

This section has students preview selected words that appear in the reading. It contains two tasks: Part A and Part B. Part A presents selected words for the students to study and learn. Part B has the students check their understanding of these words.

In Part A, the selected words are listed in three boxes. The box on the left contains words that relate to the main content area of the unit. The box on the right contains words that relate to the secondary content area of the reading. Between these two boxes are words from the reading that come from the Academic Word List (AWL). Placing the AWL words between the two lists of content area words creates a visual representation of the fact that the content area words are specific to separate content areas, while the AWL words are general academic words that might appear in either content area.

Note that the part of speech of a word is given in the chart only if this word could also be a different part of speech. Also note that some words are accompanied by words in parentheses. This alerts students to some common collocations that can form with the word and that will appear in the reading.

The vocabulary in the Vocabulary Preview is recycled over and over. The words appear in the reading; in Section 5, Vocabulary Check; in the Unit Wrap-Ups; and in the unit tests.

3 Reading

This section contains the reading and accompanying photos or illustrations. Some words from the reading are glossed at the bottom of the page. These are low-frequency words that students are not expected to know. Understanding these words might be important for understanding the reading; however, it would probably not be useful for students to incorporate the words into their active vocabulary.

The icon at the top of the page indicates that the reading is available as an MP3 file online. Students can access this by going to the *Read This!* Web site at www.cambridge.org/readthis.

4 Reading Check

This section is designed to check students' comprehension of the text. Part A checks their understanding of the main ideas. Part B asks students to retrieve more detailed information from the reading.

5 Vocabulary Check

In this section, students revisit the same vocabulary that they studied before they read the text and that they have since encountered in the reading. The Vocabulary Check contains two tasks: Part A and Part B. In Part A, students are asked to complete a text by choosing appropriate vocabulary words for the context. The text in Part A is essentially a summary of the most salient information in the reading. This activity both reinforces the target vocabulary for the chapter and the content of the reading.

Part B varies from chapter to chapter. Sometimes it has a game-like quality, where students have to unscramble a word or find the odd word out in a group of words. Sometimes the task helps students extend their understanding of the target words by working with other parts of speech derived from the words. Other times, the task tests students' knowledge of other words that the target words often co-occur with (their collocations).

6 Applying Reading Skills

An important strand of *Read This!* is reading skill development. Students are introduced to a variety of skills, such as finding main ideas and supporting details, identifying cause and effect, and organizing information from a reading into a chart. Practicing these skills will help students gain a deeper understanding of the content of the reading and the author's purpose. The section opens with a brief explanation of the reading skill and why it is important.

This section has two tasks: Part A and Part B. In Part A, students usually work with some kind of graphic organizer that helps them practice the skill and organize information. This work will prepare them to complete Part B.

7 Discussion

This section contains three questions that will promote engaging discussion and encourage students to connect the ideas and information in the readings to their own knowledge and experience. Many of the questions take students beyond the readings. There is also ample opportunity for students to express their opinions. This section helps students consolidate their understanding of the reading and use the target vocabulary from the chapter.

WRAP-UP

Each unit ends with a Wrap-Up, which gives students the chance to review vocabulary and ideas from the unit. It will also help them prepare for the unit test. (The photocopiable unit tests are to be found in the Teacher's Manual.) Teachers may want to pick and choose which parts of the Wrap-Up they decide to have students do, since to do all the activities for every unit might be overly time-consuming. The Wrap-Up section consists of the following:

Vocabulary Review. All the target vocabulary from the three chapters of the unit is presented in a chart. The chart is followed by an activity in which students match definitions to some of the words in the chart.

Vocabulary in Use. Students engage in mini-discussions in which they use some of the target language from the unit. Students will be able to draw on their personal experience and knowledge of the world.

Interview. Students work with the concepts of the readings by participating in a structured and imaginative oral activity. The interviews require that the students have understood and digested the content of at least one of the readings in a chapter. One advantage of interviews is that they are self-leveling. In other words, the sophistication of the interview is determined by the level and oral proficiency of the students. Students will need help in preparing for the interviews. They will also need time to prepare for them.

It might be a good idea for the teacher to model the first interview with one of the stronger students in the class.

Writing. This section of the Wrap-Up provides the teacher with an opportunity to have students do some writing about the content of the unit. The setup of this section varies from unit to unit.

WebQuest. For those students, programs, or classrooms that have Internet access, students can log onto www.cambridge.org/readthis. They can then find the WebQuest for the unit that they have been studying. The WebQuest is essentially an Internet scavenger hunt in which students retrieve information from Web sites that they are sent to. In this way, students encounter the information from the chapters once more. The Web sites confirm what they have already read and then broaden their knowledge of the unit topics by leading them to additional information. The WebQuests may be done individually or in pairs. Students may either submit their answers to the teacher online or they can print out a completed answer sheet and hand it in to the teacher.

Acknowledgments

Many people have been involved in the development, writing, and editing of *Read This! Intro.* I would like to thank Bernard Seal for his continued involvement in the project. His insistence on a "wow" factor in each reading has made this project a great success.

I was happy to have the opportunity to work with the talented writers Wendy Asplin, Laurie Blass, Deborah Gordon, and Mary March on this book. Likewise, our editors, Amy Cooper and Dena Daniel, and our associate managing editor, Caitlin Mara, have done an outstanding job. Thanks, too, to the production editor, Kate Spencer; the copyeditor, Kathleen Silloway; and the fact checker, Mandie Drucker. It has been fun to work with everyone on this project.

Special thanks go to Averil Coxhead for permission to cite from the Academic Word List (AWL). For the most up-to-date information on the AWL, go to http://www.victoria.ac.nz/lals/resources/academicwordlist.

I would also like to thank my colleagues and students at the University of Washington for their enthusiasm and dedication, and George and Caroline for their patience with my writing habit.

Daphne Mackey

UNIT
1
Education

Chapter 1

Late Start

Teens are too sleepy to learn early in the morning. What can schools do?

Content areas:
- Education
- Biology

Chapter 2

First Write . . . It Helps!

Sometimes students can't do their best. Psychologists can help.

Content areas:
- Education
- Psychology

Chapter 3

Student Government

In some schools, the students make all the decisions.

Content areas:
- Education
- Government

1

Late Start

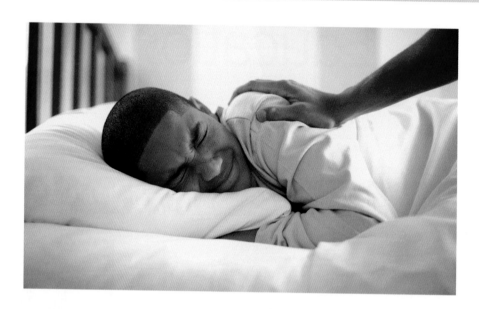

1 TOPIC PREVIEW

A People of different ages have different sleep habits. What are your sleep habits? Are they the same as your parents' or your friends' habits? Put a check (✓) in the correct column. Share your answers with your classmates.

SLEEP HABITS	ME	MY PARENTS	MY FRIENDS
1 usually sleepy by 10:00 p.m.			
2 not in bed before 12:00 a.m.			
3 usually sleep until 11:00 a.m. or 12:00 p.m. on weekends			
4 get up early in the morning and it's easy to do			

B Read the title of this chapter. Look at the picture. Then talk about these questions.

1 What time do you like to wake up in the morning? Why?

2 What is happening in the picture?

3 What do you think the reading will be about?

2 VOCABULARY PREVIEW

A Read the word lists. Which words do you know? Put a check (✓) next to them. Compare your answers with a partner. Then look up any new words in a dictionary.

Education	Academic Word List	Biology
absent drop out result (*n.*)	administrator adult grade (*n.*)	alert body clock illness tired

The chart shows some important words from the reading. These words are related to education, biology, and the Academic Word List (AWL). For more information about the AWL, see page 121.

B Fill in the blanks with words from Part A.

1 Ms. Smith's class is easy. Everyone gets a good _____ .

2 A lot of students are sick. Five of them are _____ from school today.

3 The top _____ at my school is the principal. She makes many important decisions.

4 I'm going to bed now. I feel very _____ .

5 Many young children get that _____ . They are sick for a few days, but then they get better.

6 He wants to _____ of school. He wants to get a job and save some money.

7 Go to sleep early. Then you will be _____ in class tomorrow.

8 My _____ is different from my roommate's. We always go to sleep and wake up at different times.

9 There is always one _____ on the playground with the children.

10 She swims for an hour every day. What is the _____? She can swim much faster now.

Look at the questions in Reading Check Part A on page 6. Then read the story.

Late Start

1   High schools in Minnesota have a problem. Many students are
late to school. They are often **tired**. Some students fall asleep in
class. They often get sick, too. The **administrators** think about
the problem. They make a small change. It helps a lot! What do
they do? They start the school day a little later.

2   This small change makes a big difference. Why? Most teens
are very tired early in the morning. They usually don't go to bed
until after midnight. In the morning, they wake up between
6:00 and 6:30 for school. So they don't get enough sleep. They are
still tired early in the morning. But later, teens are more awake
and ready to be in class. A later start time is better for a teen's
body clock.

3   Everyone has a body clock. An **adult's** body clock works like
this: Most adults get tired between 9:00 and 11:00 at night. They
usually go to bed before midnight. Adults can get up early in the
morning. It's not a problem. But a teen's body clock is different.
Teens don't get tired at midnight. They usually stay up later. But
early in the morning, they need more sleep.

The schools in Minnesota pay attention to the teen's body clock. They change the start of the school day from 7:20 a.m. to 8:40 a.m., 80 minutes later. Other schools in the United States change their start times, too. Some schools change the time by only 30 minutes, but they still get good **results**.

In fact, the results everywhere are amazing! More students are on time. Morning classes are easier to teach. Students are getting better **grades**. They are more **alert**. Students have fewer **illnesses**, so they are **absent** less. In Minnesota, there is another important change: Fewer students **drop out** of school or change schools. Now the students are happier, and the parents and the teachers are, too.

Today, at more and more high schools, the day is starting later. Most schools can't start two hours later. But they can change the start time a little. A small change can make a very big difference! Just ask the students.

4 READING CHECK

A Are these sentences true or false? Write *T* (true) or *F* (false).

1 _____ The students in the story are in college.

2 _____ The schools change their start times.

3 _____ The students don't like the change in start time.

B Circle the letter of the best answer.

1 What is the problem in the Minnesota schools?
   a tired students   **b** bad teachers   **c** sick teachers

2 The body clocks of teens and adults are _____ .
   a the same   **b** a little different   **c** very different

3 Many high schools start school _____ for teens' body clocks.
   a on time   **b** too early   **c** too late

4 Teens don't get enough sleep because they _____ .
   a stay up late at night
   b have bad sleep habits
   c get tired between 9:00 p.m. and 11:00 p.m.

5 Teens' body clocks tell teens to _____ .
   a go to sleep late and wake up late
   b go to sleep early and wake up late
   c go to sleep early and wake up early

6 The start time in the Minnesota schools is now _____ .
   a half an hour later
   b one hour later
   c more than an hour later

7 The students' grades are better now because _____ .
   a they are sleeping more
   b they have more time to learn
   c the classes are easier

8 The teachers are happier because _____ .
   a the teachers can sleep later
   b the administrators are happier
   c the students aren't tired anymore

5 VOCABULARY CHECK

A Retell the story. Fill in the blanks with the correct words from the box.

| absent | administrators | adults | alert | body clock |
| drop out | grades | illnesses | results | tired |

1 High school students are often very _____ in the mornings.

2 Students don't get enough sleep, so they are not _____ in their morning classes.

3 Why don't teens get enough sleep? A teen's _____ tells him or her to stay up after midnight.

4 This is not true for _____. They usually get tired between 9:00 p.m. and 11:00 p.m.

5 What are the _____ of this problem for teens?

6 In school, they don't get good _____ on their tests in early morning classes.

7 The students often don't feel well. They get different

_____ .

8 Sick students stay home. They are _____ from school.

9 Some students even _____ of school or change schools.

10 Many school _____ are changing the start times of the school day. Now there are fewer problems.

B The words *a* and *an* can go before nouns. *A* goes before consonants. *An* goes before vowels. Circle the correct word in each sentence.

1 Everybody has (a/an) body clock.

2 He is in the hospital. He has (a/an) illness called Whipple's disease.

3 (A/An) administrator makes the decisions at a school.

4 Is there (a/an) adult in the classroom with the children?

5 (A/An) result of the later start is fewer sick students at school.

6 APPLYING READING SKILLS

Finding the main idea of a paragraph is an important reading skill. Each paragraph has one main idea. It answers the question: What is this paragraph about?

A Look back at the reading, and find the correct paragraph for each main idea. Compare your answers with a partner.

MAIN IDEA	PARAGRAPH
1 There is a difference between teen and adult body clocks.	Paragraph _____
2 Minnesota high schools have a problem.	Paragraph _____
3 Even a small change can work.	Paragraph _____

B Circle the letter of the best main idea for each paragraph.

1 Paragraph 2
    a Teens are always tired in the morning.
    b Everyone has a body clock.

2 Paragraph 4
    a High schools are changing their start times.
    b Minnesota schools have an answer to the problem.

3 Paragraph 5
    a The changes bring good results.
    b Students' grades are better.

7 DISCUSSION

Talk about these questions in pairs or groups.

1 Think about your body clock. Is it more like a teen body clock or an adult body clock? Explain your answer.

2 When are you most alert? In the morning, afternoon, or evening? What do you like to do at that time of day?

3 What are some possible problems with starting the school day later?

2

First Write . . . It Helps!

1 TOPIC PREVIEW

A Is it difficult for you to do some things? Put a check (✓) next to the two most difficult activities for you. Share your answers with your classmates.

_____ give a report to the class

_____ go on a first date

_____ meet new people

_____ sing a song in front of other people

_____ take an important test

B Read the title of this chapter. Look at the picture. Then talk about these questions.

1 Which of the activities above is the most difficult for you? Why?

2 One student in the picture is standing. What is he doing? How do you think he feels?

3 What do you think the reading will be about?

2 VOCABULARY PREVIEW

A Read the word lists. Which words do you know? Put a check (✓) next to them. Compare your answers with a partner. Then look up any new words in a dictionary.

Education	Academic Word List	Psychology
information score (*n.*) study (*v.*)	file (*n.*) focus (on) (*v.*) relax stress	brain experiment (*n.*) memory

The chart shows some important words from the reading. These words are related to education, psychology, and the Academic Word List (AWL). For more information about the AWL, see page 121.

B Fill in the blanks with words from Part A.

1 Shh. You're making too much noise. I can't _____ on my book.

2 Today, scientists can look inside the _____ to see how it works.

3 Dinner with friends is a good way to _____ at the end of the day.

4 That Web site has a lot of _____ about jobs for young people.

5 She has a good _____ for people's names.

6 Put all of your homework into one _____ and e-mail it to your teacher.

7 We are doing an interesting _____ in science class today.

8 How many hours do you usually _____ math every night?

9 I can't sleep because I have a lot of _____ in my life now.

10 You cannot pass with a/an _____ of 69 percent or less.

3 READING

Look at the questions in Reading Check Part A on page 13. Then read the story.

First Write . . . It Helps!

You have an important test tomorrow. You **study** very hard. 1
You understand the **information**. You're doing well in the class.
But you're still worried. You need to **relax**. What can help?
Maybe a quiet walk? A cup of tea? A little yoga? Psychologists
have another idea: Sit down and write! Write about your **stress**.

Why does writing help? There are two reasons. First, stress 2
takes up room in the **brain**. As a result, there is less room for
memory. Writing moves the stress out of brain. It puts it on
paper. Then there is more room for memory.

Your memory works like the memory in a computer. You need 3
to delete some **files** to make room for other files. Students need
to remember a lot of information. So they need a lot of room
in their brains for memory. They need to delete their "files"
of stress.

The second reason is writing helps you to **focus**. Sometimes 4
people can think only about their stress. Writing can help them.
How? People write about their stress. As a result, they feel less
worried. Then they can focus better on other things.

5   Psychologists are studying the connection between stress and writing. They do **experiments** with students. They put students into two groups. One group of students writes about their stress for ten minutes. The other group sits quietly. Then all the students take a test. What are the results? The students in the writing group do better than the other group of students. In fact, their **scores** are one grade higher!

6   Writing can help other people, too. Some people don't sleep well. Writing at night will help them sleep better. Some athletes get stressed about winning or losing. They can't focus on playing well. Writing before a game can help them play better. People in job interviews get stressed, too. Writing before an interview can help them relax.

7   Do you get stressed about tests? Try this experiment: Go to class 10 minutes early, and write about your stress. You can write in English or your own language. Then take the test. Maybe the psychologists are right. Maybe writing will help you, too.

4 READING CHECK

A Circle the letter of the best answer.

1 _____ is a problem for many people.
   a Sitting
   b Stress
   c Information

2 Writing before a test can help you _____.
   a read better
   b sit quietly
   c relax

3 Writing about stress can help _____.
   a many people
   b psychologists
   c teachers

B Are these sentences true or false? Write *T* (true) or *F* (false).

1 _____ Students with stress can't remember important information.

2 _____ Psychologists tell us to write about happy thoughts.

3 _____ Writing can help you to focus.

4 _____ In some ways, the brain is like a computer.

5 _____ Students need to "delete" stress from their brains.

6 _____ In the experiment, some students write and some students don't.

7 _____ All the students get the same scores on the test.

8 _____ Writing at night can help people sleep less.

5 VOCABULARY CHECK

A Retell the story. Fill in the blanks with the correct words from the box.

brains	experiments	files	focus	information
memory	relaxes	scores	stress	study

1 Many students _____ hard the night before a test. They want to do well.

2 But on the day of the test, they feel a lot of _____.

3 It's difficult to _____ on the test questions.

4 The students forget a lot of important _____.

5 Stress takes up too much room in people's _____.

6 There is less room for _____.

7 Writing helps in this way: People "delete" _____ of stress and make more room to remember things.

8 Writing about stress _____ people. It makes them feel better.

9 Psychologists know this because they do _____ with groups of students.

10 What are the results? The _____ of the writing students are one grade higher.

B Some nouns and verbs have the same form. Read each sentence. Are the words underlined nouns or verbs? Circle *noun* or *verb*.

1 These psychologists don't <u>experiment</u> on animals.   noun   verb

2 The science students do many <u>experiments</u> each year.   noun   verb

3 His <u>score</u> on the quiz is very good.   noun   verb

4 I never <u>score</u> well on important tests.   noun   verb

5 I'm very tired tonight. I can't <u>focus</u> on my homework.   noun   verb

6 His <u>focus</u> is best in the afternoon.   noun   verb

6 APPLYING READING SKILLS

A Draw an arrow (→) from each cause to its effect.

CAUSE	EFFECT
1 You get stressed before a test.	**a** You make room in your brain for memory.
2 You write about your stress and put it on paper.	**b** You forget a lot of information.
3 You focus on your test.	**c** You get a better score.

B Circle the letter of the correct effect for each cause.

1 You write about your stress before an important soccer game.
   a You win the game.   **b** You play better.

2 You write about your stress at night.
   a You sleep better.   **b** You stay more alert.

3 You write about your stress before an interview.
   a You are more relaxed in the interview.   **b** You get the job.

7 DISCUSSION

Talk about these questions in pairs or groups.

1 You have an important test tomorrow. How do you feel? How does your body feel?
2 Your friend is playing in a big game tonight. She's very worried. What can you say to help her? Why will this help?
3 What are your favorite ways to relax?

3
Student Government

1 TOPIC PREVIEW

A In most schools, who makes decisions about the things below, adults or students? Write *A* (adults) or *S* (students). Share your answers with your classmates.

1 _____ school sports

2 _____ the food at school

3 _____ the start and end times of the school day

4 _____ the students' classes

5 _____ the students' clothes

B Read the title of this chapter. Look at the picture. Then talk about these questions.

1 Do you make any decisions in your English class? What do you make decisions about?

2 Who do you see in the picture? What are they doing?

3 What do you think the reading will be about?

2 VOCABULARY PREVIEW

A Read the word lists. Which words do you know? Put a check (✓) next to them. Compare your answers with a partner. Then look up any new words in a dictionary.

Education	Academic Word List	Government
budget curriculum graduate (*n.*)	administration interact	democratic govern leader rule (*n.*) vote (*v.*)

The chart shows some important words from the reading. These words are related to education, government, and the Academic Word List (AWL). For more information about the AWL, see page 121.

B Fill in the blanks with words from Part A.

1 The students _____ for the class president one time a year.

2 John has a master's degree in psychology. He is a/an _____ of Columbia University.

3 This year there is enough money in the _____ for another teacher at our school.

4 In our school, the students _____ with their teachers in class and at meals, too.

5 Our teacher made a/an _____: Don't use your cell phone in class.

6 Are both art and music part of the _____ in your school?

7 Does the _____ of your group usually start the meetings?

8 The people in the _____ are the most important people in a school. They talk about problems and make decisions at their meetings.

9 It's not easy to _____ a country. A president needs to work hard.

10 In a/an _____ country, people can choose the head of the government.

Look at the questions in Reading Check Part A on page 20. Then read the story.

Student Government

1   It's Friday morning at the Sudbury Valley School. There is a big meeting for the school **administration**. The question today is important: Can students use cell phones at school? The administrators discuss the question for 20 minutes. Then they **vote**. They vote yes!

2   Cell phones are a typical problem for schools. But this isn't a typical school meeting. What is different? Most of the administrators are not adults. They are children! They are the students. The students make decisions about everything. They help to **govern** the school.

3   Schools like Sudbury Valley are called "**democratic** schools." There are more than 30 schools like this around the world. In democratic schools, students of all ages and some adults vote on all important questions. They vote at meetings once a week. First, they talk. Then they vote. Everyone gets one vote. A student vote is as important as an adult vote. Even the vote of a five-year-old is important. There are always more students than adults in a school. So most of the votes are student votes.

What do students vote on? They vote on everything from curriculum to parties. They vote on school **rules**. They vote on the school **budget**. They even vote on the food for lunch. 4

What happens when a student breaks a rule? A special group decides. There are students and one adult in this group. These people try to understand the problem. They listen to everyone and then make decisions. They also decide on the punishment. 5

Democratic schools are not a new idea. The Sudbury Valley School is more than 40 years old. Many **graduates** of Sudbury Valley School are successful adults. Many graduates send their children to Sudbury Valley School. They want a "democratic" education for their children. 6

In some ways, Sudbury Valley School students are just like other students. They study different subjects. They learn many things. They learn to **interact** with other people. But at Sudbury Valley School, students learn other important things, too. They learn to be **leaders**. 7

4 READING CHECK

A Circle the letter of the best answer.

1 What is different about Sudbury Valley School?
   a The teachers are all very young.
   b The schools are more than 40 years old.
   c The students make important decisions.

2 Who makes the decisions at Sudbury Valley School?
   a a small group of student leaders
   b all the students and some adults
   c all the students but no adults

3 Sudbury Valley School students govern _____ of the school.
   a all parts
   b some parts
   c a few parts

B Are these sentences true or false? Write *T* (true) or *F* (false).

1 _____ Most of the administrators at Sudbury Valley School are adults.

2 _____ Students vote on food and parties, and teachers vote on other things.

3 _____ There is a special group to decide on problems with students and rules.

4 _____ Sudbury Valley School is a new type of school.

5 _____ Many Sudbury Valley School graduates send their children to Sudbury Valley School.

6 _____ Sudbury Valley School students don't learn about government.

7 _____ In Sudbury Valley School, young children's ideas are as important as adults' ideas.

8 _____ Sudbury Valley School students learn to work well with other people.

5 VOCABULARY CHECK

A Retell the story. Fill in the blanks with the correct words from the box.

administration	budget	curriculum	democratic	govern
graduates	interact	leaders	rule	vote

1 Sudbury Valley School is different from most schools because it is a/an _____ school.

2 All the students _____ on all the decisions.

3 In this way, the students _____ the school.

4 The students are part of the _____. They have meetings with the adults and make decisions.

5 But there are more students than adults, so the students are really the _____ of the school.

6 The students make decisions about the classes in the _____.

7 They also make decisions about money in the school _____.

8 Sometimes the students make a/an _____ about things like cell phone use.

9 Students and adults do many things together. At Sudbury Valley School, students _____ with the adults a lot.

10 The _____ of Sudbury Valley School know a lot about government.

B Some words go with certain prepositions. Which prepositions go with the words in bold? Circle the correct prepositions. You can look back at the reading for help.

1 The students **make decisions** (of / about / with) everything.

2 We need to **vote** (of / with / on) this year's school budget.

3 Today they will **decide** (of / on / with) the choice of food for lunch.

4 I am a **graduate** (of / on / with) Staples High School.

5 It's good to **interact** (of / with / about) people of different ages.

6 APPLYING READING SKILLS

Organizing information into a chart can help you understand the reading in a new way.

A Are these sentences true or false? Write *T* (true) or *F* (false).

1 _____ In Sudbury Valley School, students help govern their school.

2 _____ In most schools, students make important school decisions.

3 _____ In Sudbury Valley School, students often interact with people of all ages.

4 _____ In most schools, administrators decide on punishment.

5 _____ In most schools, students vote on the budget.

B Use the answers in Part A to help you complete the chart about differences between Sudbury Valley School students and students in most schools.

SUDBURY VALLEY SCHOOL STUDENTS	STUDENTS IN MOST SCHOOLS
• *help govern their school* _____	• do not help govern their school
• _____	• don't make important school decisions
• often interact with people of all ages	• _____
• decide on punishment	• _____
• _____	• don't vote on the budget

7 DISCUSSION

Talk about these questions in pairs or groups.

1 What decisions do you make in your school or at home every day?

2 Which decisions do you make alone, and which decisions do you make with other students or with other people in your family?

3 Think about your school or class. What do the teachers decide on? What does the administration decide on?

VOCABULARY REVIEW

Chapter 1	Chapter 2	Chapter 3
Education	**Education**	**Education**
absent · drop out · result (*n.*)	information · score (*n.*) · study (*v.*)	budget · curriculum · graduate (*n.*)
Academic Word List	**Academic Word List**	**Academic Word List**
administrator · adult · grade (*n.*)	file (*n.*) · focus (*v.*) · relax · stress ·	administration · interact
Biology	**Psychology**	**Government**
alert · body clock · illness · tired	brain · experiment (*n.*) · memory	democratic · govern · leader · rule (*n.*) · vote (*v.*)

Find words in the chart above that match the definitions. Answers to 1–4 are from Chapter 1. Answers to 5–8 are from Chapter 2. Answers to 9–12 are from Chapter 3.

1 Sleepy: _____

2 This person makes important decisions in a school: _____

3 To leave school forever: _____

4 Not in school on a school day: _____

5 To think hard about something: _____

6 To read notes before a test: _____

7 The amount of correct answers on a test: _____

8 You do this kind of test in a science class: _____

9 To talk, work, and do other things with people: _____

10 An amount of money to spend on something: _____

11 This tells you, "You can do this, you cannot do that": _____

12 To make all the decisions for a country: _____

VOCABULARY IN USE

Work with a partner or small group. Talk about the questions below.

1 At what age does a person become an **adult** in your culture?

2 How do you **relax** on the weekends or on vacation?

3 Who are some important **leaders** in your life? What do they lead?

4 When do you need to be very **alert** at work or in school?

5 What things do people **vote** on in your town or city?

6 What classes are in the **curriculum** at your school?

7 What does your **body clock** tell you to do at different times of day?

8 How good is your **memory**? How often do you forget things? Give examples.

INTERVIEW

Interview another student. Take turns asking and answering these questions.

1 Which story is the most interesting to you? Why?

2 Think about "First Write . . . It Helps!" How can writing help your stress? Give examples.

3 Think about "Student Government" and imagine this: You meet a Sudbury Valley School student. Talk about one similar thing and one different thing about your schools.

WRITING

In this newspaper story, there are six mistakes. Look at the example. Find five more mistakes. Then rewrite the story with the correct information.

A democratic school is opening soon. These schools are ^not^ a new idea. They are

very similar to most other schools. At democratic schools, the adults govern.

Adults make all the decisions at meetings once a year. At these meetings,

students vote on a few things. Democratic school students learn to be leaders.

A democratic school is opening soon. These schools are <u>not</u> a new idea.

WEBQUEST

Find more information about the topics in this unit. Go to www.cambridge.org/readthis and follow the instructions for doing a WebQuest. Search for facts. Have fun. Good luck!

Chapter **4**

A Strange Place to Live!

In Japan, a new type of home may help people stay young.

Content areas:
- Sociology
- Architecture

Chapter **5**

King Peggy

A woman lives two lives: a regular life in the United States, and a king's life in Africa.

Content areas:
- Sociology
- Anthropology

Chapter **6**

Quidditch: The World of Harry Potter Comes to Life

A sport goes from the bookshelf to the playing field.

Content areas:
- Sociology
- Literature

A Strange Place to Live!

1 TOPIC PREVIEW

A Look at this drawing of a living room. Is it a good room for old people? Find five things that are unsafe or difficult for old people. Circle them. Share your answers with your classmates.

B Read the title of this chapter. Look at the picture. Then talk about these questions.

1 Who is the oldest person you know? What does his or her living room look like?

2 Do you want to live to be very old? Why or why not?

3 What do you think the reading will be about?

2 VOCABULARY PREVIEW

A Read the word lists. Which words do you know? Put a check (✓) next to them. Compare your answers with a partner. Then look up any new words in a dictionary.

Sociology	Academic Word List	Architecture
elderly independent population senior (*n.*)	design (*n.*) odd	apartment balcony ceiling shape (*n.*)

The chart shows some important words from the reading. These words are related to sociology, architecture, and the Academic Word List (AWL). For more information about the AWL, see page 121.

B Fill in the blanks with words from Part A.

1 Her mother is 75. She's a/an _____ .

2 My grandparents' house is too big for them now. They're moving to a/an

_____ .

3 The window is in the _____ of a circle.

4 There are so many people in Tokyo! In fact, it has the largest

_____ of any city in the world.

5 Houses usually are one color, but my friend's house is purple, pink, blue,

and green. That's very _____!

6 I don't like the _____ of that house. It's too modern
and unusual.

7 This room has yellow walls. Look up! The _____
is pink!

8 It's a beautiful sunny day! Let's have lunch outside on the

_____ .

9 _____ people usually walk more slowly than
young people.

10 He doesn't like to ask for help from anybody. He's very

_____ .

Look at the questions in Reading Check Part A on page 30. Then read the story.

A Strange Place to Live!

1   Everyone looks twice at one **apartment** building in Mitaka, Japan. On the outside, the apartments are like toy blocks.[1] They are pink, purple, yellow, and other bright colors. They have **shapes** like circles and squares. It's a very **odd** building.

2   Do you want to see more? Walk inside one of the apartments. Be careful! Don't fall! The floors are not flat. It's hard to keep your balance.[2] Do you want to see the **balcony**? Watch out! Don't hit your head! The door to the balcony is very small. It's very low. You have to crawl[3] through it. Do you want to look out the window? Good luck! One window is up near the **ceiling**. Another

---

[1] *blocks:* small squares made of wood or plastic; children use them to build things

[2] *keep your balance:* not fall over when you stand or walk

[3] *crawl:* move forward on your hands and knees

window is down near the floor. There are no closets. Everything about this apartment is unusual!

Why do people want to live in this odd place? The answer is surprising. This unusual **design** is good for you! It keeps your brain active. It keeps your body active, too. You have to work to keep your balance. You have to reach up and bend down a lot. This exercise is healthy, especially for **elderly** people. 3

The architects are Shusaku Arakawa and Madeline Gins. They have unusual ideas. They don't want to make comfortable, relaxing apartments for older people. Arakawa says, ". . . you'll live better, longer and even forever" in these apartments. 4

Many **seniors** don't want to live here. They don't like the unusual design. They don't want to fall. They like flat floors. They don't want unusual doors and windows. They want light colors on the walls. They want to feel comfortable in their old age! 5

But some seniors want to live in the apartments. They don't want to live with their children or in a home for old people. They like to be **independent**. They don't want to relax. They want to stay active. These odd apartments help them feel young. 6

These apartments are very unusual. But there is a good reason for the design. The **population** in many countries is growing older. Maybe someday this kind of design will help elderly people all over the world. Maybe it will help them be active and independent. 7

4 READING CHECK

A Are these sentences true or false? Write *T* (true) or *F* (false).

1 ____ The design of the apartments is very unusual.

2 ____ The apartments are for elderly people to live in.

3 ____ A person can relax and be comfortable in them.

B Circle the letter of the best answer.

1 Why do people look twice at the apartment building in the reading?
   a It makes people feel younger.
   b It has many colors and shapes.
   c It has many windows.

2 The floors are ____.
   a not flat
   b odd shapes
   c easy to walk on

3 Which sentence is true?
   a Some windows are near the floor.
   b All the windows are near the ceiling.
   c There are no windows.

4 Which sentence is true?
   a You walk through a window to go to the balcony.
   b You crawl through a door to go to the balcony.
   c You cannot go onto the balcony.

5 Why do some people want to live in the apartments?
   a The apartments are not expensive.
   b The apartments give them exercise.
   c The architects are famous.

6 Why *don't* some people want to live in the apartments?
   a They like bright colors on the walls better.
   b They like buildings with odd shapes better.
   c They like comfortable apartments better.

7 What is the reason for the design of the apartments?
   a You can relax there.
   b You can live longer there.
   c You can have fun there.

5 VOCABULARY CHECK

A Retell the story. Fill in the blanks with the correct words from the box.

apartment	balcony	design	elderly
independent	odd	population	shapes

Everyone stops and looks at one _____ building in
Japan. It is very _____. It has unusual
                     2
_____ and colors, like toy blocks. The door to the
         3
_____ is very small and low. It looks like a place for
         4
children, but it is a home for _____ people. The architects
                                5
have a reason for the unusual _____. They say old people
                                6
need difficult homes. Difficult homes will keep their bodies and
brains active.

The _____ in many countries is growing older. Maybe
            7
this kind of living space will help older people be more
_____ and healthy for a longer time.
         8

B Make a word from the story. Put the letters in parentheses ( ) in the correct
order. Write the word in the sentence.

1 Architects _____design_____ buildings. (segnid)

2 It's nice to sit on the _____ in nice weather. (cyanblo)

3 He's old and doesn't work. He's a _____. (nisoer)

4 Japan, like many countries, has a large elderly _____.
   (touppnolia)

5 Many elderly people don't want to live with their children. They prefer to
   be _____. (deneptinend)

6 There is a very high _____ in the room. (glincei)

6 APPLYING READING SKILLS

Organizing information into a chart can help you see the information in a reading in a new way. This can give you a deeper understanding of the reading.

A Which sentences describe Arakawa and Gins' apartments? Put a check (✓) next to them.

_✓_ They have rooms with very bright colors.

_____ They have rooms with flat floors.

_____ They have windows in the middle of the wall.

_____ They are easy to walk in.

_____ They have windows near the floor.

_____ They have very small doors.

_____ They have balconies with regular doors.

B How are regular apartments different from Arakawa and Gins' apartments? Put the information from Part A in the correct columns. Then add one more piece of information to each column.

REGULAR APARTMENTS	ARAKAWA AND GINS' APARTMENTS
have flat floors	*have very bright colors*

7 DISCUSSION

Talk about these questions in pairs or groups.

1 Think about an elderly person you know. Do you think he or she wants to live in an Arakawa and Gins apartment? Why or why not?
2 In your opinion, what are the good things about an Arakawa and Gins apartment? What are the bad things?
3 What can people do to live longer lives?

1 TOPIC PREVIEW

A A *monarchy* is a system of government. The leader is a king or queen. What do you know about monarchies? Put a check (✓) next to the true sentences. Share your answers with your classmates.

_____ Saudi Arabia has a monarchy.

_____ Some monarchies only have a king, never a queen.

_____ When a king or queen dies, the people usually choose a new leader.

_____ There are monarchies in Asia.

_____ A monarchy is a new system of government, less than a hundred years old.

_____ Today, no country has a queen.

B Read the title of this chapter. Look at the picture. Then talk about these questions.

1 What women leaders do you know about?

2 Who do you think is better as a leader, a woman or a man? Explain your answer.

3 What do you think the reading will be about?

2 VOCABULARY PREVIEW

A Read the word lists. Which words do you know? Put a check (✓) next to them. Compare your answers with a partner. Then look up any new words in a dictionary.

Sociology	Academic Word List	Anthropology
female **in charge** (of) **relative** **respect** (*n.*)	**assist** **traditionally**	**elder** (*n.*) (perform a) **ritual** **royalty** **tribe**

The chart shows some important words from the reading. These words are related to sociology, anthropology, and the Academic Word List (AWL). For more information about the AWL, see page 121.

B Fill in the blanks with words from Part A.

1 _____, women in the United States wear white on their wedding day.

2 Her job is to _____ the queen. She plans meetings and gives the queen important information.

3 In most cultures, parents teach their children to have _____ for adults.

4 In her anthropology class, she is studying the Maasai _____. The Maasai are a group of people in Kenya.

5 His family comes from France. When he visits Paris, he doesn't need a hotel. He stays with a/an _____.

6 Some women feel more comfortable with a/an _____ doctor.

7 I am the president of the company. I'm _____ of all the workers.

8 Her new husband is a prince. She is _____ now. She's a princess!

9 That old man knows all about our history. He is a/an _____. He makes many decisions for our people.

10 Women in Ethiopia perform a coffee _____ every morning. They do it exactly the same way every time.

Look at the questions in Reading Check Part A on page 37. Then read the story.

King Peggy

Peggy Bartels is asleep in her apartment near Washington, D.C. It is 4:00 a.m. The telephone rings. The caller is a **relative** from Otuam in Ghana, West Africa. He has bad news. Peggy's elderly uncle, the king of Otuam, is dead. The caller also has good news for Peggy. She is the new king!   1

Peggy is very surprised. Why is she the new king? She is not the king's only relative. There are many other relatives in the **tribe** in Otuam. Also, she is a woman. **Traditionally**, kings are men.   2

Peggy's tribe has a special way to decide on a new king. The **elders** of the tribe meet and perform a **ritual**. They say the names of all the king's relatives and wait for a sign. When they say Peggy's name, they see a sign. At first, they don't believe it. They say her name two more times. They see the sign again both times. The answer is clear to the elders. Peggy is their new king.   3

After three sleepless nights, Peggy accepts. She becomes the first **female** king of Otuam: King Nana Amuah-Afenyi VI, or King Peggy.   4

Now Peggy has two lives. She still lives in the United States most of the year. She lives in a one-bedroom apartment. She goes   5 out to eat in restaurants. She drives an old car. Peggy works in an office.[1] She **assists** her co-workers with their work.

6   Peggy travels to Ghana on her vacations. In Otuam, she stays in a palace[2] with eight bedrooms. Kings traditionally don't eat in restaurants, so she has a chef[3] in the palace. She also has a driver to take her places.

7   In Otuam, Peggy is **in charge** of the government. She decides how to spend the village's money. Peggy assists people in Otuam, too. She helps the people of her tribe have a better life. In fact, her next plan is to build a high school in the village.

8   In the United States, people call her "Peggy." In Otuam, people call her "Nana." *Nana* is a word of **respect**. It is for important people, and Peggy is *very* important in Otuam. She is **royalty**!

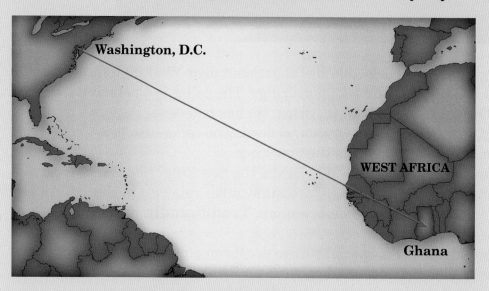

---

[1] She works in the embassy of Ghana, the office of the Ghana government in the United States.

[2] *palace:* the large house of a king or queen

[3] *chef:* a professional cook

4 READING CHECK

A Match the person to the action.

1 _____ Peggy's uncle

2 _____ King Peggy

3 _____ Peggy Bartels

a lives in a one-bedroom apartment in the United States

b died in Otuam

c is in charge of the government in Otuam

B Circle the letter of the best answer.

1 When does Peggy get the telephone call from her relative?
  a in the morning   **b** in the afternoon   **c** in the evening

2 Where is Ghana?
  a the United States   **b** South America   **c** West Africa

3 What news surprises Peggy?
  a She is the new king.
  b Her relative is calling her.
  c Her uncle is a king.

4 The elders choose Peggy because _____ .
  a they want a female king
  b they see a sign
  c she is the king's only relative

5 Which sentence is *not* true about Peggy's life in the United States?
  a She drives an old car.
  b She lives in an apartment.
  c She is in charge of the government.

6 What does Peggy want to do in Otuam?
  a build a high school
  b eat in public
  c stay in an apartment

7 Why do people call Peggy "Nana" in Otuam?
  a Peggy is an American.
  b Peggy is important.
  c Peggy assists people.

5 VOCABULARY CHECK

A Retell the story. Fill in the blanks with the correct words from the box.

assists	elders	female	in charge	relative
respect	ritual	royalty	traditionally	tribe

1 Peggy gets a call from a/an _____ in Otuam, Ghana, very early in the morning.

2 He has sad news. The leader of their _____, Peggy's uncle, is dead.

3 He also tells her some surprising news. The _____ want her to be the new king.

4 This is a surprise because, _____, the king is a man.

5 In Otuam, the people perform a/an _____. They say the name of each relative and wait for a sign.

6 They see a sign and choose Peggy. She is the first _____ king of Otuam.

7 She has two lives now. In Washington, D.C., she _____ people with their work.

8 In the United States, she is a regular person. But in Otuam, she is _____.

9 She makes important decisions. She is _____ of the government, and she decides how to spend its money.

10 The people of Otuam have a lot of _____ for her. They call her "Nana."

B Read the four words. Which word does *not* belong? Cross it out.

1 uncle   relative   daughter   queen

2 tribe   king   people   group

3 female   sign   elders   ritual

4 usually   never   traditionally   commonly

5 palace   bedroom   apartment   respect

6 APPLYING READING SKILLS

Understanding the order of events is an important reading skill. You can make a list to help you.

A Make a list to show Peggy's story. Write the events in the correct order from 1 (first event) to 5 (last event).

- Peggy accepts the job of king.

- Peggy gets a phone call at 4:00 a.m.

- The king of Otuam dies.

- The caller tells Peggy she is the new king.

- The elders choose Peggy as their new king.

1	*The king of Otuam dies.*
2	
3	
4	
5	

B Read these steps in the ritual. Number them in the correct order from 1 to 5.

_____ **a** The elders say Peggy's name two more times.

_____ **b** The elders say the names of all the king's relatives.

_____ **c** The elders meet to choose a new king.

_____ **d** The elders choose Peggy as the new king.

_____ **e** The elders say Peggy's name and see a sign.

7 DISCUSSION

Talk about these questions in pairs or groups.

1 What are some ways to choose a leader?
2 Do you think Peggy is a good choice for a king? Why or why not?
3 Peggy lives in two different cultures. What are some good things and some bad things about her life?

6

Quidditch: The World of Harry Potter Comes to Life

1 TOPIC PREVIEW

A What do you think of sports? Circle the words in bold to make the sentences true for you. Share your answers with your classmates.

1 I think sports are **fun** / **boring**.

2 I like to **play** / **watch** sports.

3 I am **good** / **bad** at sports.

4 I like **team sports, like soccer** / **individual sports, like tennis**.

5 I **have** / **don't have** a favorite sport.

6 I **have** / **don't have** a favorite team.

B Read the title of this chapter. Look at the picture. Then talk about these questions.

1 What movie does the picture make you think of? What are the people in the picture doing?

2 What do you know about the game of quidditch?

3 What do you think the reading will be about?

2 VOCABULARY PREVIEW

A Read the word lists. Which words do you know? Put a check (✓) next to them. Compare your answers with a partner. Then look up any new words in a dictionary.

Sociology	Academic Word List	Literature
compete event (have) **in common** movement reality	media reaction	character fiction novel

The chart shows some important words from the reading. These words are related to sociology, literature, and the Academic Word List (AWL). For more information about the AWL, see page 121.

B Fill in the blanks with words from Part A.

1 My wife and I have tickets to the Superbowl! It's the biggest American football _____ of the year!

2 His brother likes to run in races, and he also likes to travel. So he always tries to _____ in races in different cities and countries.

3 Who is your favorite _____ in the Harry Potter books? My favorite is Professor Dumbledore.

4 We both like to dance, go to movies, and play tennis. We have a lot _____ .

5 Many children today don't eat very well. There is a/an _____ in the school system to improve school lunches.

6 Look at all the reporters and photographers! The _____ follow this movie star everywhere.

7 The movie is interesting, but it's not a true story. It doesn't show _____ .

8 I think the first Harry Potter _____ is the writer's best book. I want to read it again.

9 Sometimes real life is stranger than _____ .

10 What is your _____ to the new sports Web site? Do you think it's good or bad?

3 READING

Look at the questions in Reading Check Part A on page 44. Then read the story.

Quidditch: The World of Harry Potter Comes to Life

1   In New York City, a large park is very busy. This is a big **event**! The **media** are there. More than 700 college students are **competing** on 46 teams. The team from Middlebury College[1] wins 1st prize. Yale[1] is 16th. The students from Harvard[1] don't do very well. They are too slow on their broomsticks.[2]

2   Broomsticks? That's right. This is not a soccer competition. This is the Quidditch World Cup! Do you know quidditch? It's a sport in the Harry Potter **novels** and movies. But now, **fiction** is **reality**.

3   The year is 2005. A group of college students in Vermont wants to have some fun. Some like to play sports. Some don't like sports at all. But they have one interest **in common**. They all love Harry Potter.

4   The students decide to play quidditch. They make rules and a scoring system.[3] Soon, other students want to play, too. News

---

[1] *Middlebury College, Yale, Harvard:* three universities in the United States
[2] *broomstick:* the long handle of a broom

[3] *scoring system:* a way to count points in a game

about the game spreads through the Internet. More and more students want to play. Today, there are more than 500 quidditch teams around the world!

Quidditch for real people is hard to play. Harry Potter and his team fly on broomsticks. But try to run with a broomstick between your legs! Players have to "ride" the broomstick during the whole game. They fall down a lot! 5

At Quidditch World Cup events, people want to win, but they also want to have fun. Fans sell T-shirts. Some dress as Harry Potter **characters**. The winning team gets a big trophy[4] – a big *plastic* trophy! 6

People have different **reactions** to quidditch. Some people say, "It's just a silly game." But many people say, "This is a serious sport." There is an international group called the IQA (International Quidditch Association). There are Web sites and even a magazine. There is also a **movement** to make quidditch a national sport in the United States. Who knows? Maybe quidditch will be an Olympic event in the future! 7

Sports bring people together for fun, exercise, and friendship. This is true for any sport. But fans of quidditch are not just making friends. They're making history. For the first time, literature is helping to make a new sport! 8

---

[4] *trophy:* a prize for winning

4 READING CHECK

A Circle the letter of the best answer.

1 Quidditch is a ____ .
   a character in a book
   b new sport
   c name of a college

2 Where does quidditch come from?
   a sports teams in New York City
   b college students from Yale and Harvard
   c the Harry Potter books and movies

3 Why is quidditch difficult to play in real life?
   a The players have to dress as Harry Potter characters.
   b The players have to use broomsticks.
   c The game doesn't have any rules.

B Are these sentences true or false? Write *T* (true) or *F* (false).

1 ____ At the competition in New York City, soccer teams are competing for a trophy.

2 ____ The Harvard team wins first prize.

3 ____ "Real" quidditch begins in 2005 with college students in Vermont.

4 ____ The Vermont quidditch players all love the Harry Potter stories.

5 ____ Today, there are more than 700 quidditch teams around the world.

6 ____ The players don't care about winning the competition.

7 ____ The winning team gets a T-shirt.

8 ____ Some people want to make quidditch a national sport in the United States.

9 ____ Quidditch is a new Olympic event.

10 ____ Quidditch is the only sport that comes from literature.

5 VOCABULARY CHECK

A Retell the story. Fill in the blanks with the correct words from the box.

character	event	in common	media
movement	novels	reality	

1 The Quidditch World Cup is an international sporting _____ in New York City.

2 A large park is very busy. Fans, friends, and the _____ are all there to see it.

3 Quidditch is a sport in the Harry Potter _____ .

4 Harry Potter is the main _____ in the famous books and movies.

5 The quidditch players have something _____ . They all love Harry Potter.

6 Quidditch is in a story. Now it is also _____ .

7 Many people like this new sport. In fact, there is a/an _____ to make quidditch a national American sport.

B Choose the correct form of the word to complete each sentence.

1 compete (*v.*)   competitive (*adj.*)   competition (*n.*)

   a Sports teams have fun, but they are very _____ , too.

   b The Olympics are an international sports _____ .

   c Teams from all over the world _____ in the Olympics.

2 fiction (*n.*)   fictional (*adj.*)

   a Some people prefer biographies and other true stories. I like to read _____ . Those stories are not real.

   b Harry Potter is a _____ character. Daniel Radcliffe plays him in the movies.

3 reaction (*n.*)   react (*v.*)

   a People _____ differently to quidditch. Some people like it, and some people think it's silly.

   b What is your _____ to the Harry Potter movies? Do you think they're as good as the books?

6 APPLYING READING SKILLS

Sometimes you need to find some information quickly. **Scanning** *means looking quickly to find the information. First ask yourself, "What type of information am I looking for?"*

A Check (✓) the box for the type of information you are looking for: a name of a person, a name of a place, a number, or a date. Then scan to find the information in the reading, and underline it.

	NAME OF A PERSON	NAME OF A PLACE	A NUMBER	A DATE
New York City				
46				
2005				
Harry Potter				
700				
Middlebury College				

B Scan the reading "Quidditch: The World of Harry Potter Comes to Life" on pages 42–43. Find this information.

1 The name of a character in novels and movies: _____

2 The year quidditch for real people starts: _____

3 The number of teams in the Quidditch World Cup: _____

4 The city with the Quidditch World Cup: _____

5 The winner of the competition: _____

6 The number of college students at the big quidditch event:

_____

7 DISCUSSION

Talk about these questions in pairs or groups.

1 Why do you think so many people like quidditch?
2 Do you think quidditch is silly or serious?
3 What sports are common in your culture? Do you think quidditch is a good sport for your culture?

VOCABULARY REVIEW

Chapter 4	Chapter 5	Chapter 6
Sociology	**Sociology**	**Sociology**
elderly · independent · population · senior (n.)	female · in charge (of) · relative · respect (n.)	compete · event · (have) in common · movement · reality
Academic Word List	**Academic Word List**	**Academic Word List**
design (n.) · odd	assist · traditionally	media · reaction
Architecture	**Anthropology**	**Literature**
apartment · balcony · ceiling · shape (n.)	elder (n.) · (perform a) ritual · royalty · tribe	character · fiction · novel

Find words in the chart above that match the definitions. Answers to 1–4 are from Chapter 4. Answers to 5–8 are from Chapter 5. Answers to 9–12 are from Chapter 6.

1 Strange: _____

2 The top of a room: _____

3 The way a building or product looks: _____

4 Not in need of any help to do something: _____

5 Kings and queens: _____

6 To help or support: _____

7 A member of your family: _____

8 A group of people with the same history and culture: _____

9 A feeling about something new: _____

10 To try to do better than other people at something: _____

11 Newspapers, magazines, and television: _____

12 A long story in book form: _____

VOCABULARY IN USE

Work with a partner or small group. Talk about the questions below.

1 Who is your favorite **character** in any **novel**? Why?

2 Do you ever see someone **perform a ritual**? Describe it.

3 What are some types of **media**?

4 Think about these **shapes**: circle, square, rectangle, triangle. Draw a picture of a person. Use only these shapes.

5 What kind of **apartment** do you want to live in? Describe it.

6 Do you know an **elderly** person? Who is it, and what is interesting about him or her?

7 What is your favorite **event** in the Olympics? Why?

8 What job do you want to do in the future? What do you want to be **in charge of**? Why?

INTERVIEW

Interview another student. Take turns asking and answering these questions.

1 Which story is the most interesting to you? Why?

2 Think about "King Peggy." Imagine you are a king. You want to help your people. How do you help them?

3 Think about "A Strange Place to Live!" Imagine you are living in one of the apartments. Your friends want to visit you. What do you tell them before they visit you?

WRITING

This is a summary of one of the readings in this unit. The sentences are not in the correct order. Rewrite the summary. Put the sentences in the correct order.

They all love Harry Potter. They make up rules and a scoring system. Today there are more than 500 quidditch teams around the world! A group of college students in Vermont wants to have some fun. The students decide to play quidditch. More and more students want to play.

WEBQUEST

Find more information about the topics in this unit. Go to www.cambridge.org/readthis and follow the instructions for doing a WebQuest. Search for facts. Have fun. Good luck!

UNIT

3

Science

Chapter 7

Rescue in Chile

Thirty-three men need help! They are 2,200 feet under the ground in a mine, and they can't get out.

Content areas:
- Science
- Engineering

Chapter 8

Sleeping Beauty

A teenage girl has an unusual problem. She sleeps for weeks.

Content areas:
- Science
- Medicine

Chapter 9

Memory Palace

Some people have amazing memories! How do they remember so much?

Content areas:
- Science
- Education

Rescue in Chile

1 TOPIC PREVIEW

A Which person has the most dangerous job? Number the jobs from *1* (most dangerous) to *5* (least dangerous). Share your answers with your classmates.

_____ farmer

_____ firefighter

_____ miner

_____ police officer

_____ teacher

B Read the title of this chapter. Look at the picture. Then talk about these questions.

1 What things do we get from mines?
2 What does this picture show?
3 What do you think the reading will be about?

2 VOCABULARY PREVIEW

A Read the word lists. Which words do you know? Put a check (✓) next to
them. Compare your answers with a partner. Then look up any new words in
a dictionary.

Science	Academic Word List	Engineering
dig mineral oxygen surface	device finally survive	diagram drill (*n.*) shaft

The chart shows some important words from the reading. These words are related to science, engineering,
and the Academic Word List (AWL). For more information about the AWL, see page 121.

B Fill in the blanks with words from Part A.

1 You use a/an _____ to make a hole in something hard.

2 The boy does not go down into the mine. He stays up on the

_____ .

3 The miners walk down a long _____ to get into
the mine.

4 She wants to plant a tree. First, she needs to _____ a
hole in the ground.

5 People need food and water to _____ .

6 Gold is a/an _____ . Silver is, too.

7 Most people have a cell phone. It is a very common

_____ .

8 People need _____ to live. It's a gas in the air.

9 This _____ shows the design of the building. The doors
will be here. The stairs will be there.

10 It takes hours to make this cake, but it's _____ ready
to eat.

Look at the questions in Reading Check Part A on page 54. Then read the story.

Rescue in Chile

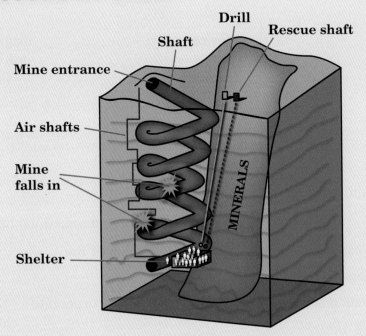

1   Thirty-three men are in a small, dark place. It is 2,200 feet (670 meters) under the ground. The men are miners, and they are trapped¹ in a mine. They are alive, but does anyone know? Suddenly, they hear a noise. It's a **drill**! It is making a hole in the rock. Someone on the **surface** is trying to find the miners. But then the sound stops. The men hear the drill six times. It gets close, but then it goes away. Will anyone rescue them?

2   The story begins on August 5, 2010, in Chile. Thirty-three miners go to work. They go down a **shaft** deep into the ground. There, they **dig** for **minerals**. At first, it's a regular day. Then in seconds, everything changes. Part of the mine falls in. The men cannot get out.

3   The miners are safe. But they are in a very small space. It is only 540 square feet (50 square meters). They only have a little food. They are afraid. How long will the food last? Will they have enough **oxygen**?

---

¹ *trapped:* not able to get out or escape

Above the mine, engineers begin to work. They look at a diagram of the mine. Then they start to drill holes. They drill for days, but they find nothing. Maybe the miners are dead. Then after 17 days, they hear a sound. Tap. Tap. Tap. Someone is tapping on the drill! When they pull the drill out, it has a note on it. It says, "We are fine. There are 33 of us. We are all alive."

4

Everyone is very happy, but there is bad news, too. The rescue will take months. How can 33 men live in such a small place for a long time? Many countries want to help. They send many things for the rescue. They also send small electronic devices. The miners can use these devices to talk to their families. They can also watch videos. They watch a soccer game. The players' shirts say "Miners be strong!"

5

Many engineers work on the rescue. A special drill makes a new shaft. A rescue pod[2] will go down the shaft to bring each miner up. The pod is only 21 inches wide (53 centimeters).

6

Finally, the shaft is complete. On October 12, after 68 days, the first miner comes up to the surface. All over the world, people watch. Everyone cheers! Twenty-two hours later, everyone is still cheering. The last miner finally gets to the top! All 33 **survive**.

7

[2] *rescue pod:* a long narrow container

4 READING CHECK

A Match the amount of time to the action.

1 seconds _____   **a** The miners stay in the mine.

2 weeks _____   **b** Part of the mine falls in.

3 months _____   **c** No one knows if the miners are alive.

B Are these sentences true or false? Write *T* (true) or *F* (false).

1 _____ The miners are trapped under the ground.

2 _____ One of the miners is a woman.

3 _____ The mine is in Chile.

4 _____ The sound of the drill is good news for the miners.

5 _____ It is difficult to live in a very small place for a long time.

6 _____ Other countries send shirts to the miners.

7 _____ The engineers use an old shaft for the rescue.

8 _____ The engineers use a very large rescue pod to bring the miners up.

9 _____ The miners all come up to the surface at the same time.

10 _____ All the men survive.

5 VOCABULARY CHECK

A Retell the story. Fill in the blanks with the correct words from the box.

devices	diagram	dig	drill	finally
minerals	oxygen	shaft	surface	survive

1 In Chile, there are many _____ under the ground in a mine.

2 Miners _____ in the mine. It's their job. But one day, part of the mine falls in. The miners are trapped.

3 Of course, they are afraid. Do they have enough food? Is there enough _____ ?

4 They hear the sound of a/an _____ . Someone is trying to find them!

5 Engineers look at a/an _____ of the mine.

6 After 17 days, the engineers _____ find the miners.

7 The engineers send small electronic _____ down to the miners.

8 The engineers make a new _____ to reach the miners.

9 After more than three months, the first miner comes up to the _____ .

10 All 33 miners _____ .

B Some nouns and verbs have the same form. Read each sentence. Are the words in bold nouns or verbs? Circle *noun* or *verb*.

1 Do you have a <u>drill</u>?   noun   verb

2 We need to <u>drill</u> a hole here.   noun   verb

3 The engineers <u>are drilling</u> a new shaft to reach the miners.   noun   verb

4 The miners hear the sound of a <u>drill</u>.   noun   verb

5 This device <u>drills</u> through rock.   noun   verb

6 The engineers use <u>drills</u> to find the miners.   noun   verb

6 APPLYING READING SKILLS

*Sometimes you need to find some information quickly. **Scanning** means looking quickly to find the information. First ask yourself, "What type of information am I looking for?"*

A Check (✓) the box for the type of information you are looking for: a name, a number, or a date. Then scan to find the information in the reading and underline it.

	A NAME	A NUMBER	A DATE
2,200			
670			
August 5, 2010			
Chile			
Thirty-three			
540			
50			

B Scan the reading "Rescue in Chile" on pages 52–53, and find this information.

1 the number of miners _____

2 the country _____

3 the size of the rescue pod _____

4 the date of the rescue _____

5 the number of days in the mine _____

7 DISCUSSION

Talk about these questions in pairs or groups.

1 What do you think? How do the miners feel in the mine?
2 Do you know of any other rescues? Talk about them.
3 Why do people take dangerous jobs?

CHAPTER

8

Sleeping Beauty

1 TOPIC PREVIEW

A Some people sleep more, other people sleep less. Which sentences are true for you? Put a check (✓) next to them. Share your answers with your classmates.

1 _____ I sleep for 5 or 6 hours a night.

2 _____ I sleep for 7 or 8 hours a night.

3 _____ I sleep for 9 or 10 hours a night.

4 _____ I usually get enough sleep each night.

5 _____ I am often tired in the daytime because I don't get enough sleep at night.

B Read the title of this chapter. Look at the picture. Then talk about these questions.

1 Do you often get less sleep than you need? If so, how do you feel?

2 How old is the person in the picture? What is she doing?

3 What do you think the reading will be about?

2 VOCABULARY PREVIEW

A Read the word lists. Which words do you know? Put a check (✓) next to them. Compare your answers with a partner. Then look up any new words in a dictionary.

Science	Academic Word List	Medicine
rare symptom temperature	affect (*v.*) normal period	condition cure (*n.*) diagnose virus

The chart shows some important words from the reading. These words are related to science, medicine, and the Academic Word List (AWL). For more information about the AWL, see page 121.

B Fill in the blanks with words from Part A.

1 Two minutes is a short _____ of time.

2 He has a heart _____ . It's very bad. He needs to use oxygen.

3 Most people sleep for eight hours. This is _____ .

4 Does cold weather _____ you in any way?

5 Only a few people have this illness. It's very _____ .

6 It's cold today. The _____ is 32°F (0°C).

7 She has a sore throat. This is usually a/an _____ of a cold.

8 Scientists are trying to find a/an _____ for that illness.

9 The doctor will give you some tests to help _____ your problem.

10 Sometimes a/an _____ lasts only 24 hours. Then you feel better the next day.

Look at the questions in Reading Check Part A on page 61. Then read the story.

Sleeping Beauty

One day, Louisa Ball is a **normal** teenager. The next day, her 1
life is not normal at all. Why? She goes to sleep, and she can't
wake up. Her parents say, "Please get up. Please have something
to eat." Louisa does not move. She does not even open her eyes.
She does not wake up until days later. Then she goes back to her
normal life. But soon Louisa is asleep again.

Most teenagers do not get enough sleep. Louisa gets *too much* 2
sleep. In fact, sometimes Louisa sleeps for almost two weeks.
Her parents try to wake her. She needs to eat and wash. Louisa
gets out of bed and walks, but she isn't really awake. She is
sleepwalking. Later, she remembers nothing.

Some people call Louisa "Sleeping Beauty," but her life is not a 3
fairy tale.[1] Her friends go to parties. Her family takes vacations.
Louisa is not with them. She is asleep. She also sleeps through
important things like tests at school. She is not doing well in
her classes.

---

[1] *fairy tale:* a story for children; it usually has a happy ending

4   What is wrong with Louisa? At first, no one knows. She doesn't have a cold. Her **temperature** is normal. Some people say, "There's nothing wrong with her." "She needs to get up and go to school." Finally, the doctors **diagnose** her problem. Louisa has Kleine-Levin Syndrome (KLS). KLS is a **rare** brain **condition**. Only about 1,000 people in the world have it. Most people with KLS are teenagers. They sleep for long **periods** of time. Some people sleep for months. There is no **cure** for KLS.

5   Doctors don't know the exact cause of KLS. Maybe a **virus** is the cause. In fact, Louisa had a virus just before her first long period of sleep.

6   Louisa knows the **symptoms** of KLS. She feels unhappy. She gets mad easily. She stops talking to her friends. She needs to go home. She needs to go to bed.

7   Louisa's life stops for weeks because of KLS. But there is some good news for her. KLS does not last forever. It usually **affects** people for 8 to 12 years. Louisa will probably have a normal life again someday. She and her family are hopeful. Maybe that day will come soon.

Louisa Ball

4 READING CHECK

A Are these sentences true or false? Write *T* (true) or *F* (false).

1 _____ Louisa Ball's life is not normal.

2 _____ Louisa does not get enough sleep.

3 _____ Louisa will always have this problem.

B Circle the letter of the best answer.

1 Why is Louisa's life difficult?
  a She doesn't like her friends and family.
  b She can't do things with her friends and family.
  c She wants to do things with her friends and family.

2 How long does Louisa sometimes sleep?
  a for years
  b for months
  c for more than a week

3 What does Louisa remember when she wakes up?
  a She remembers nothing.
  b She remembers eating.
  c She remembers everything.

4 What is a problem for Louisa?
  a She sleeps through important things.
  b Some people call her "Sleeping Beauty."
  c Sometimes she does not get enough sleep.

5 Which sentence is true about KLS?
  a The cause is a virus.
  b A lot of people have KLS.
  c Doctors do not know the cause.

6 Which group does KLS affect most?
  a people in their 20s   **b** teenagers   **c** 8- to 12-year olds

7 What is *not* a symptom of KLS for Louisa?
  a She needs to go to sleep.
  b She wants to see her friends.
  c She gets angry and unhappy.

8 Louisa's life will probably be normal in about _____.
  a 5 years   **b** 10 years   **c** 20 years

5 VOCABULARY CHECK

A Retell the story. Fill in the blanks with the correct words from the box.

affects	condition	cure	diagnoses	normal
periods	rare	symptoms	temperature	virus

1 What's wrong with Louisa? She doesn't have a cold, and her
_____ is fine. It's 98.6° F (37° C).

2 Finally, a doctor _____ her problem.

3 Louisa has Kleine-Levin Syndrome. KLS is a brain
_____ .

4 People with KLS sleep for long _____ of time.

5 No one knows the cause of KLS, but some people have a/an
_____ first.

6 There is no _____ for KLS.

7 Only about 1,000 people in the world have KLS. It is very
_____ .

8 KLS usually _____ teenagers.

9 Louisa knows the _____ of KLS. She gets mad easily,
and she feels very tired.

10 Louisa wants a/an _____ life soon. But people usually
have KLS for about 10 years.

B Make a word from the story. Use the definitions to put the letters in the
correct order.

1 _____*cure*_____ a way to end an illness   reuc

2 _____ not common   erra

3 _____ amount of time   idepro

4 _____ an illness   inooidcnt

5 _____ not unusual   roanlm

6 _____ find out the cause of an illness   gadisone

6 APPLYING READING SKILLS

*Main ideas are the most important information in a reading. Supporting details tell you more about the main ideas. **Finding main ideas and supporting details** will help you understand a reading better.*

A Match the main ideas of the reading with the supporting details. Write the letter of each detail in the correct box.

MAIN IDEA	SUPPORTING DETAILS
1 Louise Ball's life is not normal. ☐ ☐	**a** Most people with KLS are teenagers. **b** Louisa sleeps for days. **c** Only about 1,000 people in the world have KLS. **d** Louisa can't do things with her family and friends.
2 KLS only affects some people. ☐ ☐	

B Find two supporting details for this main idea in the reading.

There is some good news for Louisa.

_____

_____

7 DISCUSSION

Talk about these questions in pairs or groups.

1 Think about life with KLS. What is the most difficult part?

2 Some teens have KLS for many years. What problems do they have? What parts of life do they sleep through?

3 Can people with KLS be successful later in life? Why or why not?

Memory Palace

1 TOPIC PREVIEW

A There are 52 cards in a deck of cards.[1] Can you mix the cards up and then remember the order? Put a check (✓) next to the true sentences. Share your answers with your classmates.

1 _____ I can probably remember the order of 5 cards in a deck.

2 _____ I can probably remember the order of 10 cards in a deck.

3 _____ I can probably remember the order of 15 cards in a deck.

4 _____ I can probably remember the order of all 52 cards in a deck.

5 _____ I probably can't remember the order of any cards in a deck.

B Read the title of this chapter. Look at the picture. Then talk about these questions.

1 Are you good at memory tests? Do like memory games? Give an example.
2 What is happening in the picture? What are they doing?
3 What do you think the reading will be about?

---

[1] *deck of cards:* you use a deck of cards to play games

2 VOCABULARY PREVIEW

A Read the word lists. Which words do you know? Put a check (✓) next to them. Compare your answers with a partner. Then look up any new words in a dictionary.

Science	Academic Word List	Education
human mind	mental researcher visual	ability correctly memorize practice (*v.*) recall

The chart shows some important words from the reading. These words are related to science, education, and the Academic Word List (AWL). For more information about the AWL, see page 121.

B Fill in the blanks with words from Part A.

1 A/An _____ studies things and tries to find new information.

2 It is difficult to _____ a lot of new words at one time.

3 He never uses the word *their* _____ . He always writes *there* instead of *their*.

4 She reads very quickly. This _____ is helpful in school.

5 She is taking a great science class. Her _____ is full of new ideas.

6 A/An _____ has a larger brain than a bird.

7 She wants to play the piano well. She needs to _____ every day.

8 He has a very bad memory. He can't _____ her name.

9 I can't remember names, but I never forget a face. I have very good _____ memory.

10 Some doctors help people with physical problems. Other doctors help people with _____ problems.

MP3 **3** READING

Look at the questions in Reading Check Part A on page 68. Then read the story.

Memory Palace

1   It's the last day of the World Memory Championship.[1] About 30 people sit at tables. "Ready? Begin!" Each person picks up a deck of cards. The cards are not in order. For example, the first card is the queen of hearts. Next is the 10 of diamonds. Each person needs to **memorize** the order of all 52 cards.

2   After 46 seconds, 14-year-old Katharina Bunk puts down her cards. Now comes the memory test. Each person gets a new deck of cards. Everyone needs to put the cards in this deck in the same order as the cards in the first deck. Does Katharina memorize the order **correctly**? Yes! She is the new memory champion.

3   How do memory champions like Katharina memorize things so quickly? Brain **researchers** know the answer. Memory champions use a different part of the brain to memorize. They use **visual** memory. They see pictures in their **minds**. Maybe

---

[1] *championship:* a competition to find the best team or player in a game or sport; a *champion* is the winner of a competition

Katharina sees the cards in the kitchen. The queen of hearts is cooking. The 10 of diamonds is sitting at the table.

Every person isn't a memory champion. But most people have good visual memory. They remember places that they see. Why? Scientists have an idea: **Humans** needed this **ability** in the past. They needed to remember places with food or shelter.[2] 4

We can all use visual memory to remember information. We imagine a place in our minds. Then we add details to the place. This **mental** picture is called a memory palace. 5

You can **practice**. First, choose a place. It can be any place, such as your home or school. This is your memory palace. Next, imagine the inside of the place. Maybe you see a door, a hall, and a picture on the wall. Remember these things. They will help you later. 6

For example, maybe you want to remember to buy a pen, a notebook, and some paper today. Add pictures of these things to your memory palace. Imagine an action for each one. 7

- A large pen is opening the front door.
- A notebook is walking down the hall.
- Some paper is falling out of the picture onto the floor.

Now imagine a walk through your memory palace. At the store, walk through the memory palace in your mind again. You will **recall** the pen, the notebook, and the paper very easily! 8

Wang Feng

Remember Katharina Bunk, the 14-year-old? Now 46 seconds seems slow. Wang Feng is the new winner. He memorizes the deck of cards in 24 seconds! He doesn't walk through a memory palace – he runs! 9

---

[2] *shelter:* a place of protection from bad weather or danger

4 READING CHECK

A Circle the letter of the best answer.

1 Katharina Bunk can _____ .
   a read numbers very quickly
   b memorize things very quickly
   c play card games very well

2 A memory palace is _____ .
   a a real place
   b a way to remember things
   c a house from the past

3 Most humans have good _____ memory.
   a physical
   b mental
   c visual

B Are these sentences true or false? Write *T* (true) or *F* (false).

1 _____ Katharina Bunk is the Memory Champion of China.

2 _____ Katharina Bunk memorizes 52 cards in 46 seconds.

3 _____ Scientists study the brains of memory champions.

4 _____ Everyone uses the same part of the brain to memorize things.

5 _____ Humans needed visual memory to survive a long, long time ago.

6 _____ You can buy a memory palace to help you.

7 _____ Mental pictures help you remember.

8 _____ Katharina Bunk is not the memory champion now.

9 _____ Wang Feng has a bad memory.

10 _____ Wang Feng memorizes 52 cards in 24 minutes.

5 VOCABULARY CHECK

A Retell the story. Fill in the blanks with the correct words from the list.

ability	correctly	humans	memorize	mental
minds	practice	recall	researchers	visual

1 In the World Memory Championship, first people need to
_____ the order of a deck of cards.

2 Katharina Bunk finishes and gets a new deck. Now she needs to
_____ the order of the first deck of cards.

3 Can she do it _____? Yes! She is the winner!

4 Brain _____ study memory champions.

5 Memory champions use _____ memory.

6 They make pictures in their _____ .

7 These _____ pictures help them remember things.

8 In the old days, _____ needed to remember places to
find food and shelter.

9 These days we still use this human _____ to
remember things.

10 You can do it, too. But you need to _____ . It takes time
to learn to use a memory palace.

B Which word goes with the two words on the left? Circle *a* or *b*.

1 mental   brain   **a** correctly   **b** mind

2 scientists   information   **a** researcher   **b** visual

3 recall   remember   **a** mental   **b** memorize

4 picture   see   **a** visual   **b** correctly

6 APPLYING READING SKILLS

Understanding the order of events is an important reading skill. You can make a list to help you.

A Make a list to show the steps in the memory championship. Write the steps in the correct order from *1* to *7*.

- They memorize the order of the cards.

- Someone checks the order of the second deck.

- They get a second deck of cards.

- The people sit at tables.

- They put down the cards.

- They put the second deck in the same order as the first deck.

- They pick up a deck of cards.

1 *The people sit at tables.*
2
3
4
5
6
7

B Number these steps in the correct order from *1* to *5*. They explain how to use a memory palace.

_____ **a** Walk through your memory palace again later. You will recall everything.

_____ **b** Practice one time. Imagine a walk through the memory palace.

_____ **c** Imagine actions for each thing in your memory palace.

_____ **d** Choose a place for your memory palace.

_____ **e** Imagine the inside of your memory palace.

7 DISCUSSION

Talk about these questions in pairs or groups.

1 When can a memory palace help you?
2 How do you usually memorize a lot of information? Give an example.
3 What kind of jobs will Wang Feng and Katharina Bunk probably be good at?

VOCABULARY REVIEW

Chapter **7**	Chapter **8**	Chapter **9**
Science	**Science**	**Science**
dig · mineral · oxygen · surface	rare · symptom · temperature	human · mind
Academic Word List	**Academic Word List**	**Academic Word List**
device · finally · survive	affect (*v.*) · normal · period	ability · mental · researcher · visual
Engineering	**Medicine**	**Education**
diagram · drill (*n.*) · shaft	condition · cure (*n.*) · diagnose · virus	correctly · memorize · practice (*v.*) · recall

Find words in the chart above that match the definitions. Answers to 1–4 are from Chapter 7. Answers to 5–8 are from Chapter 8. Answers to 9–12 are from Chapter 9.

1 After a long time: _____

2 A machine that makes a hole in something hard: _____

3 To make a hole in the ground: _____

4 The top; the outside of something: _____

5 How hot or cold something is: _____

6 To find out the cause of a medical problem: _____

7 Very unusual: _____

8 An illness or a medical problem: _____

9 With no mistakes: _____

10 A person, not an animal: _____

11 This person tries to find information: _____

12 To remember: _____

VOCABULARY IN USE

Work with a partner or small group. Talk about the questions below.

1. Are you a **visual** learner? Do you need to see something to learn it?

2. Do you and your family have the same **abilities**? For example, can you all sing or draw well?

3. How do you usually **memorize** new words?

4. What are the **symptoms** of a cold?

5. What is a **cure** for a sore throat?

6. Do you ever get too much sleep? How does this **affect** you?

7. Which **device** is more important to you, a phone or a music player? Why?

8. How long can someone **survive** with no **oxygen**?

INTERVIEW

Interview another student. Take turns asking and answering these questions.

1. Which story is the most interesting to you? Why?

2. Think about "Rescue in Chile" and imagine this: You are one of the miners. You are waiting for help. How do you spend your time?

3. Think about "Sleeping Beauty" and imagine this: You are Louisa's doctor. You diagnose her condition. Now you are talking to her parents. What do you say?

WRITING

In this newspaper story about one of the readings, there are eight mistakes. Look at the example. Find seven more mistakes. Then rewrite the story with the correct information.

17

After ~~27~~ days, there is good news from the mine in Argentina. The 42 miners are alive! They are in a large place in the mine. It is 2,200 feet above the ground. Engineers in the mine are working on the rescue. A large rescue pod will go up the shaft.

After 17 days, there is good news from the mine . . .

WEBQUEST

Find more information about the topics in this unit. Go to www.cambridge.org/readthis and follow the instructions for doing a WebQuest. Search for facts. Have fun. Good luck!

Chapter 10

FarmVille

A computer game helps to
sell real food!

Content areas:
- Marketing
- Computer Studies

Chapter 11

Guerilla Marketing

Is it art or is
it advertising?

Content areas:
- Marketing
- Art and Design

Chapter 12

The Land of Poyais

A ship took 243 people
to a place called Poyais.
What happened?

Content areas:
- Marketing
- Travel and Tourism

1 TOPIC PREVIEW

A How do you learn about things to buy? Put a check (✓) next to the
true sentences.

1 _____ I see things to buy on TV.

2 _____ I see things to buy on the Internet.

3 _____ I read about things to buy in magazines.

4 _____ My friends talk about things to buy.

5 _____ _____ (your idea)

B Read the title of this chapter. Look at the picture. Then talk about
these questions.

1 Where do you often see this type of picture?

2 What do you see in the picture? Does the picture show something to buy?
If so, what is it?

3 What do you think the reading will be about?

2 VOCABULARY PREVIEW

A Read the word lists. Which words do you know? Put a check (✓) next to them. Compare your answers with a partner. Then look up any new words in a dictionary.

Marketing	Academic Word List	Computer Studies
advertise brand customer product sales	awareness goal target (*v.*)	click on online

The chart shows some important words from the reading. These words are related to marketing, computer studies, and the Academic Word List (AWL). For more information about the AWL, see page 121.

B Fill in the blanks with words from Part A.

1 You can read the news in the newspaper or _____ on your computer.

2 How do you start this computer game? Just _____ the "Play" button.

3 She has one important _____ this year: to save money for a new car.

4 Many people like to work on a laptop computer. It's a useful

_____ .

5 My favorite _____ of laptop computer is the Apple MacBook.

6 He buys many things at that store. He's a good _____ .

7 The food company is making a lot of money now. Their

_____ are going up.

8 Many companies like to _____ on TV and in magazines.

9 The students are learning a lot about saving money.

_____ about money is very important.

10 Teenage males usually drink a lot of cola, so the Coca-Cola company

wants to _____ this type of person.

Look at the questions in Reading Check Part A on page 78. Then read the story.

FarmVille

1   The Cascadian Farms company sells food **products**. The company has a big problem. Most people don't know about it. It needs a place to **advertise**.

2   Zynga is another company. It makes **online** games. The company's **goal** is to "connect people with their friends through games." Zynga has the answer to Cascadian Farms' problem. It's a game called FarmVille.

3   In this game, the players work on a farm. They grow food and raise animals. They even earn virtual[1] money. About 20 million people play FarmVille every day. The average FarmVille player is between 20 and 40 years old, and more than half of the players are women. This is great for Cascadian Farms! It **targets** the same type of person!

4   Cascadian Farms and Zynga have a deal. The food company pays Zynga to put Cascadian Farms products in the FarmVille game. The game works like this: Players **click on** Cascadian Farms. Then they start to grow Cascadian Farms fruit. Why? The players can make a lot of money with Cascadian Farms fruit.

---

[1] *virtual:* on a computer, not part of the real world

FarmVille players learn about the Cascadian Farms **brand**. Then, in a real grocery store, they see Cascadian Farms products. They try them. Then they buy more. They become good **customers**, and Cascadian Farms' **sales** go up. 5

This kind of advertising is called *product placement*. It's not really new. For example, think about the movies. You see a strong, handsome man on the screen. He is driving a BMW very fast. He drives home and turns on his computer. The computer is an Apple product. He is thirsty. He goes into the kitchen and opens the refrigerator. He takes out a can of Coke. Are the BMW, Apple, and Coca-Cola companies just lucky? No. They pay a lot of money to advertise in the movie. 6

Now a lot of companies place their products in online games. Does this type of advertising work? Yes! FarmVille helped Cascadian Farms increase their brand **awareness** by 550 percent. That's a lot of real-life customers! 7

4 READING CHECK

A Match the phrases to make true sentences.

1 FarmVille is _____ .

2 Cascadian Farms is _____ .

3 Product placement is _____ .

a a way to advertise

b a food company

c an online game

B Circle the letter of the best answer.

1 Cascadian Farms needs _____ .
   a more products
   b more virtual money
   c more places to advertise

2 The Zynga company _____ .
   a makes games
   b sells food
   c grows food

3 Cascadian Farms have a deal with _____ .
   a FarmVille
   b Zynga
   c BMW

4 Most FarmVille players are _____ .
   a women
   b men
   c farmers

5 FarmVille players _____ .
   a grow food
   b cook food
   c find money

6 You see product placement in _____ .
   a refrigerators
   b cars
   c movies

7 Why does Cascadian Farms advertise in FarmVille?
   a They want to teach players about their products.
   b They want to earn virtual money.
   c They want to help Zynga.

5 VOCABULARY CHECK

A Retell the story. Fill in the blanks with the correct words from the list.

advertise	awareness	brand	click on	customers
goal	online	products	sales	target

1 Many companies use product placement to _____ things.

2 We often see a/an _____ like Coca-Cola in the movies.

3 Companies are advertising in _____ games, too.

4 Zynga's _____ is to connect people with their friends through games.

5 In the game, players _____ Cascadian Farms and start to grow Cascadian Farms fruit.

6 After the game, players have a/an _____ of Cascadian Farms products.

7 They buy Cascadian Farms food in real stores, so they become good

_____ .

B Some nouns and verbs have the same form. Read each sentence. Are the underlined words nouns or verbs? Circle *noun* or *verb*.

Noun	Verb
product	produce
sales	sell
target	target

1 Zynga <u>produces</u> online games.   noun   verb

2 Fruit is one of Cascadian Farms' <u>products</u>.   noun   verb

3 Cascadian Farms' <u>sales</u> are going up.   noun   verb

4 Cascadian Farms <u>sells</u> more fruit now.   noun   verb

5 The drink company <u>targets</u> young people.   noun   verb

6 Women are the <u>target</u> of the advertising.   noun   verb

6 APPLYING READING SKILLS

Organizing information in a chart can help you understand the reading in a
new way.

A Who does what and why? Fill in the *What?* column to complete the chart.
Write each phrase in the correct place.

work on a virtual farm   play FarmVille
needs to advertise   makes online games

WHO?	WHAT?	WHY?
Cascadian Farms		to increase people's awareness of their products
Zynga		to connect people through games
People		to have fun
Players		to earn virtual money

B Look back at the reading to complete the information in this chart.

WHO?	WHAT?	WHY?
FarmVille players		to make a lot of money
FarmVille players		to try Cascadian Farms products
The BMW, Apple, and Coca-Cola companies		to advertise their products

7 DISCUSSION

Talk about these questions in pairs or groups.

1 Do you play online games? Why or why not?
2 Is product placement in online games a good idea or a bad idea? Explain
   your answer.
3 Give some more examples of product placement. What products do you see
   on TV, in movies, and in online games?

11

Guerilla Marketing

1 TOPIC PREVIEW

A Read the sentences about advertising. Do you agree? Write *Y* (yes) or *N* (no).

1 _____ I always read advertising.

2 _____ I sometimes read advertising.

3 _____ I never read advertising.

4 _____ Advertising is never interesting.

5 _____ Advertising is sometimes interesting.

6 _____ Advertising is always interesting.

B Read the title of this chapter. Look at the picture. Then talk about these questions.

1 What do you see in the picture?
2 Is there advertising in the picture? If so, what does it tell you to buy?
3 What do you think the reading will be about?

2 VOCABULARY PREVIEW

A Read the words. Which words do you know? Put a check (✓) next to them. Then work with a partner. Look up the new words in a dictionary.

Marketing	Academic Word List	Art and Design
ad (advertisement) **cheap** **message**	**equipment** **location** **unique**	**artistic** **graffiti** **imagination** **sculpture**

The chart shows some important words from the reading. These words are related to marketing, art and design, and the Academic Word List (AWL). For more information about the AWL, see page 121.

B Fill in the blanks with words from Part A.

1 This is an unusual car. It's _____ because it's different from all the other cars.

2 There is a good _____ for a new car in this magazine. It shows a big picture of the car.

3 She is a very _____ person. She makes beautiful pictures of flowers.

4 There is a big _____ of a bird in the park. It's a beautiful work of art.

5 Some people think _____ is art. Other people do not like to see these words and pictures in public places.

6 The car costs a lot of money. It's not _____!

7 His company sells _____ for cooking, like pots and pans.

8 This sign sends a/an _____ to customers. It tells them to buy the products.

9 Advertising is everywhere. Sometimes it's in an unusual _____, such as a subway car.

10 You need a lot of _____ to be a writer or an artist.

Look at the questions in Reading Check Part A on page 85. Then read the story.

Guerilla Marketing

Imagine this: You're parked in a parking lot. You want to leave, 1
but you can't. Another car is right behind you. There's a note
on the car window. It says: "Sorry, I had to run. Feel free to get
inside and move the car." You see the keys are inside! You move
the car. Then you find out: This is an **ad** for a car company. It's
another way to say, "Please try the car." And you just did! This is
an example of guerilla marketing.

Guerilla marketing is a **unique** way to advertise for very 2
little money. It's usually very surprising or unusual. It often
uses everyday **locations**, such as streets, sidewalks, and walls.
Sometimes the advertisements are even in buses and trains!
Guerilla marketing sends a **message**, and it's often **artistic**, too.
Here are some more examples:

You're on the subway. The train starts to move. You reach up to 3
hold the bar so you don't fall. The bar is actually a large weight
from the gym! It looks like you're lifting it! It's amazing! Then
you see the ad for a health and fitness club.

4   You're crossing the street. You look down. There's a barbecue grill¹ in the street! It looks like an interesting **sculpture**. Then you see the writing: It's an ad for a barbecue **equipment** company. The company used a hole in the street to advertise its products!

5   You're walking in town. Suddenly, you see some letters and words on the ground. The letters and words look very artistic. Did a **graffiti** artist put them there? You stop and read the words. No, it is not art. The words say: "ASDA. Saving You Money Every Day." ASDA is a supermarket, and this is an ad.

6   Why do companies love guerilla advertising? It's **cheap** and it works. All they need are some inexpensive materials and a lot of **imagination**. So the next time you see something unusual in the street or on the bus, look again. Maybe it's a guerilla ad!

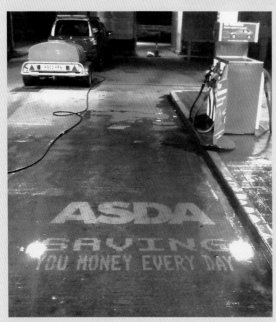

¹ *barbecue grill:* something to cook food on outdoors. The word *barbecue* is sometimes written *BBQ*.

84   Unit 4 Marketing

4 READING CHECK

A Are these sentences true or false? Write *T* (true) or *F* (false).

1 _____ Guerilla marketing is a type of art.

2 _____ Guerilla marketing is unusual.

3 _____ Guerilla marketing is cheap.

B Circle the letter of the best answer.

1 What is the goal of the car ad?
a you leave a note
b you take the car home
c you try the car

2 Guerilla marketing uses _____.
a unusual locations
b everyday locations
c artistic locations

3 You probably don't see guerilla marketing _____.
a on the sidewalk
b on the subway
c on TV

4 What is the subway ad for?
a candy   **b** health food   **c** a gym

5 Where is the barbecue equipment ad?
a in the street
b on the subway
c on a sculpture

6 What does the supermarket ad look like?
a dirt   **b** graffiti   **c** money

7 Which sentence describes guerilla marketing?
a It isn't expensive.
b It isn't artistic.
c It isn't unique.

8 What does guerilla marketing need?
a imagination
b expensive materials
c a lot of equipment

5 VOCABULARY CHECK

A Retell the story. Fill in the blanks with the correct words from the list.

ads	artistic	cheap	equipment	graffiti
imagination	locations	message	sculptures	unique

1 Guerilla _____ are unusual.

2 You can see guerilla ads in everyday _____ , such as on subways and sidewalks.

3 They are also very _____ , but an artist doesn't usually make them.

4 Sometimes you see words on the street. They look like _____ , but they are not. They are selling a product.

5 Sometimes these ads are big objects like birds or animals. They look like _____ .

6 Different companies use guerrilla ads: a health club, a barbecue _____ company, and a supermarket.

7 They are sending a/an _____ about their products.

8 People with a lot of ideas and _____ make the ads.

B Make a word from the story. Put the letters in parentheses ( ) in the correct order. Write the word in the sentence.

1 Guerilla ads are in interesting _____ , such as on the street. (caonslito)

2 Guerilla ads are _____ . They don't cost a lot of money. (paceh)

3 The company sells weights and other gym _____ . (temniuqpe)

4 You need a lot of _____ to make guerrilla ads. (nigitomanaii)

5 The car ad is _____ . You don't see other ads like it. (uqneiu)

6 APPLYING READING SKILLS

Asking and answering "Why?" questions about a reading helps you develop critical thinking skills. In other words, it helps you think carefully about the ideas.

A Look at the reading to find the answers to these "Why?" questions. Compare your answers with a partner.

Why did the note in the car say, "Feel free to get inside and move the car"

Why is guerilla marketing unique

Why is guerilla marketing cheap

B Practice using "Why?" questions. Write two more "Why?" questions about the reading. Then ask and answer the questions with a partner.

1 Why _____

_____

2 Why _____

_____

7 DISCUSSION

Talk about these questions in pairs or groups.

1 What is your favorite guerilla ad in this chapter? Why?
2 Is guerilla marketing a good idea or a bad idea? Explain your answer.
3 Imagine your own guerilla ad for a product. Describe it. What does it sell? How does it sell it?

12
The Land of Poyais

1 TOPIC PREVIEW

A What are some reasons to move to a new country? Number the reasons
from *1* (most important) to *5* (least important). Then add your own idea.
Share your answers with your classmates.

1 _____ There is good land for farms.

2 _____ There are a lot of jobs.

3 _____ There are big cities with a lot of buildings.

4 _____ There are beautiful beaches.

5 _____ _____ (your idea)

B Read the title of this chapter. Look at the picture. Then talk about
these questions.

1 What do you see in the picture?
2 Is this a good place to live? Why or why not?
3 What do you think the reading will be about?

2 VOCABULARY PREVIEW

A Read the word lists. Which words do you know? Put a check (✓) next to them. Compare your answers with a partner. Then look up any new words in a dictionary.

Marketing	Academic Word List	Travel and Tourism
campaign promise (*n.*) publicity	area persuade resources	destination tourist traveler trip

The chart shows some important words from the reading. These words are related to marketing, travel and tourism, and the Academic Word List (AWL). For more information about the AWL, see page 121.

B Fill in the blanks with words from Part A.

1 She visits a different country every year. She is a world

_____ .

2 He didn't go to Mexico to live; he just went there for a visit. He's a/an

_____ .

3 El Salvador has many natural _____ , such as water
and good land for farming.

4 He tried to _____ her to go to Mexico with him, but she
was too busy.

5 This plane is going to Central America. The _____
is Belize.

6 We had a great _____ to India last fall. We saw a lot of
interesting things, and we met nice people.

7 Her new book about Japan is getting a lot of _____ in
newspaper articles and magazine ads.

8 The company made a/an _____ : If you don't like our
product, you will get your money back.

9 The hotel is in a nice _____ . It's near the beach.

10 The advertising _____ was very successful. Many
people learned about the company on TV and in newspaper ads.

Look at the questions in Reading Check Part A on page 92. Then read the story.

The Land of Poyais

1   "Come to Poyais. Start a new life!" the advertisement said. "Poyais is a wonderful place. It has beautiful beaches. The capital city has banks, an opera house, and a cathedral.[1] You will enjoy delicious food from local farms. You will love the place!"

2   Many people in Great Britain heard about Poyais. Two hundred and forty-three people decided to go there. These people were not **tourists**. They bought land in Poyais. They planned to stay there forever.

3   The people left Britain in 1823. They sailed on ships for many weeks. Finally they arrived at their **destination**. The ship left the people on an empty beach. They looked around. There was a big problem. There was no city, no farmland. There was nothing but insects.

4   Why didn't these poor **travelers** find the beautiful land of Poyais? There was a good reason: Poyais didn't exist! A man named Gregor MacGregor invented the place.

5   MacGregor was from Scotland. He always wanted to be rich, so he became a pirate.[2] In 1820, he sailed along the coast of Central America.

---

[1] *cathedral:* a large, important church
[2] *pirate:* a person who attacks ships and steals from them

MacGregor stopped in a swampy³ **area**. He met the local chief, 6
and they became friends. The chief gave MacGregor some land.

Gregor MacGregor

MacGregor named the land Poyais. Then he went back to Britain. He had an idea: Sell land in Poyais to the British. He started a big marketing **campaign**. The campaign was full of **promises**: Poyais is a perfect world! Plants grow quickly! There are many valuable **resources**! There is gold! There's a big capital city with beautiful buildings! MacGregor even invented an army and Poyais money.

Important people in Britain believed MacGregor. Newspapers 7
wrote about Poyais. This gave MacGregor even more **publicity**.
The publicity **persuaded** many people about the wonderful
land. For example, rich people bought Poyais land. By 1823,
MacGregor was a millionaire.

Then it was time for the first people to move to Poyais. They 8
changed all their English money for Poyais money. They were

Poyais money

full of hope on the **trip**. But Poyais was a terrible surprise. It was impossible to live there.

What happened to 9
those people on the beach? People from a country nearby rescued them.

Some of the people stayed in Central America. Others went back
to Britain. All were sad and very poor.

People in Great Britain learned the truth about MacGregor's 10
false advertising. MacGregor didn't go to jail, but he had to leave
the country. His destination? Not Poyais! He lived the rest of his
life in Venezuela.

---

³ *swampy:* describes very wet and soft land

4 READING CHECK

A Are these sentences true or false? Write *T* (true) or *F* (false).

1 _____ Poyais was a real country.

2 _____ Many people moved to Poyais.

3 _____ Gregor MacGregor told the truth about Poyais.

B Circle the letter of the best answer.

1 Poyais was in _____ .
   a Great Britain
   b Central America
   c North America

2 How did MacGregor get Poyais?
   a A chief sold it to him.
   b A chief invented it for him.
   c A chief gave it to him.

3 Which sentence tells the truth about Poyais?
   a There are buildings and farms.
   b There are insects and swamps.
   c There are resources such as gold there.

4 How did MacGregor get rich?
   a He sold British land to people.
   b He found gold in Poyais.
   c He sold Poyais land to British people.

5 When did people learn the truth about Poyais?
   a on the ships
   b after they went there
   c before they went there

6 How many people went to Poyais?
   a 234
   b 243
   c 423

7 What happened to MacGregor?
   a He went to jail.
   b He went to Venezuela.
   c He stayed in Great Britain.

5 VOCABULARY CHECK

A Retell the story. Fill in the blanks with the correct words from the box.

area	campaign	destination	persuaded	promises
publicity	resources	tourists	travelers	trip

1 Gregor MacGregor started a big marketing _____ to advertise Poyais.

2 The ads were full of _____. They said, "Poyais is a wonderful place. You will love it."

3 "It has lots of _____ such as gold, and it has good farmland."

4 There was a lot of _____ about Poyais in the newspapers.

5 The ads _____ a lot of people to go to Poyais.

6 In 1823, 243 _____ got on a ship to go to Poyais.

7 They weren't _____. They planned to move to Poyais and live there.

8 On the _____, they were hopeful and excited.

9 After many weeks, they got to their _____. It was a bad surprise.

10 All they saw was a swampy _____.

B Which word goes with the two words on the left? Circle *a* or *b*.

1 trip   traveler   **a** beach   **b** tourist

2 campaign   advertising   **a** publicity   **b** area

3 traveler   destination   **a** pirate   **b** tourist

4 land   area   **a** destination   **b** gold

5 sell   persuade   **a** promise   **b** resources

6 APPLYING READING SKILLS

Events in a reading happen in order from the first event to the last event.
Understanding the order of events *is an important reading skill. You can make a list to help you.*

A Make a list to show the story of Poyais. Write the events in the correct order from *1* (first event) to *5* (last event).

- MacGregor went back to Great Britain and advertised Poyais.

- MacGregor met a chief and got some land.

- MacGregor got an idea: Invent Poyais and sell Poyais land.

- MacGregor became a pirate.

- MacGregor went to the coast of Central America.

1 *MacGregor became a pirate.*
2
3
4
5

B Read the rest of the events in the story about Poyais. Number them in the correct order from *1* to *6*.

_____ **a** Some people went home, and others stayed in Central America.

_____ **b** Many people believed the publicity.

_____ **c** The people got to Poyais and learned the truth.

_____ **d** More than 200 people sailed to Poyais.

_____ **e** There was a lot of publicity about Poyais.

_____ **f** Many people bought Poyais land.

7 DISCUSSION

Talk about these questions in pairs or groups.

1 Are most ads true or false? Explain your answer.
2 What is the best way to persuade people to go to a place?
3 Think of an ad for your favorite place. What does it say?

UNIT
4
WRAP-UP

VOCABULARY REVIEW

Chapter **10**	Chapter **11**	Chapter **12**
Marketing	**Marketing**	**Marketing**
advertise · brand · customer · product · sales	ad (advertisement) · cheap · message	campaign · promise (*n.*) · publicity
Academic Word List	**Academic Word List**	**Academic Word List**
awareness · goal · target (*n.*)	equipment · location · unique	area · persuade · resources
Computer Studies	**Art and Design**	**Travel and Tourism**
click on · online	artistic · graffiti · imagination · sculpture	destination · tourist · traveler · trip

Find words in the chart above that match the definitions. Answers to 1–4 are from Chapter 10. Answers to 5–8 are from Chapter 11. Answers to 9–12 are from Chapter 12.

1 Using the Internet: _____

2 This person buys things: _____

3 To tell people about a product or a service: _____

4 Knowing about something: _____

5 Writing and pictures in public places: _____

6 A place: _____

7 Not expensive: _____

8 You use this to think of new and interesting ideas: _____

9 This person visits a place for fun: _____

10 "Yes, I will surely do it today." is an example of this: _____

11 You get there at the end of your trip: _____

12 Useful things in a place, such as water or minerals: _____

VOCABULARY IN USE

Work with a partner or small group. Talk about the questions below.

1 What is **unique** about your city or town? Explain your answer.

2 What are your **goals** for this year?

3 What are some of your favorite **brands**? Why do you like them?

4 What is your favorite **ad**? Describe it. Why do you like it?

5 Did you ever **persuade** a friend to do something? Explain your answer.

6 Where did you go on your last **trip**? Describe the place.

7 Are you a **traveler**? Or do you like to stay home? Explain your answer.

8 Do you like **sculpture**? Why or why not?

INTERVIEW

Interview another student. Take turns asking and answering these questions.

1 Which story is the most interesting to you? Why?

2 Think about "Guerilla Advertising" and imagine this: You see the car with the note. What do you do? Do you move the car? Why or why not?

3 Think about "The Land of Poyais" and imagine this: You live in Britain in 1823. You read an ad for Poyais. Do you believe it? Why or why not?

WRITING

Read the sentences about "FarmVille." Put them in the correct order from 1 (first) to 6 (last). Then write the sentences in a paragraph to tell the story.

_____ **a** They learn all about the Cascadian Farms brand.

_____ **b** The players can grow Cascadian Farms fruit on the farm.

_____ **c** The players work on a farm and earn virtual money.

_____ **d** Farmville is an online game.

_____ **e** Cascadian Farms is happy because their sales are going up.

_____ **f** Then the players become Cascadian Farms customers in real stores.

WEBQUEST

Find more information about the topics in this unit. Go to www.cambridge.org/readthis and follow the instructions for doing a WebQuest. Search for facts. Have fun. Good luck!

UNIT

5

TV and Film Studies

Chapter 13

Mean Judges

Sometimes, we like mean people. Why is this true?

Content Areas:
- TV and Film Studies
- Sociology

Chapter 14

The Uncanny Valley

How can a happy children's movie make us uncomfortable? One researcher has the answer.

Content Areas:
- TV and Film Studies
- Psychology

Chapter 15

A New Language

Someone made a movie about an unusual world. The characters speak a new language there.

Content Areas:
- TV and Film Studies
- Language Studies

Mean Judges

1 TOPIC PREVIEW

A Many people watch contests on TV. How about you? Put a check (✓) next to the true sentences. Share your answers with your classmates.

1 _____ I like to watch contests on TV.

2 _____ I listen to the judges.

3 _____ I like to guess the winner.

4 _____ I want to be in a TV contest.

5 _____ I don't watch contests on TV.

B Read the title of this chapter. Look at the picture. Then talk about these questions.

1 In TV contests, someone always loses. Do you usually feel good or bad about the loser? Why?

2 Who do you see in the picture? What are they doing?

3 What do you think the reading will be about?

2 VOCABULARY PREVIEW

A Read the word lists. Which words do you know? Put a check (✓) next to them. Compare your answers with a partner. Then look up any new words in a dictionary.

TV and Film Studies	Academic Word List	Sociology
audience contestant reality TV tune in TV viewer	expert status style	behavior popular

The chart shows some important words from the reading. These words are related to TV and film studies, sociology, and the Academic Word List (AWL). For more information about the AWL, see page 121.

B Fill in the blanks with words from Part A.

1 Every day, people _____ to the news on television.

2 He knows all about Latin American songs. He's a/an _____ in Latin American music.

3 Movies about animals are very _____ . Many people enjoy them.

4 On _____ shows, you see real people, not actors.

5 During the funny part of the movie, everyone in the _____ laughed.

6 In a singing contest, each _____ sings a song.

7 He is a normal _____ . He watches TV for three hours every day.

8 In most countries, a professor is an important person. The job has a lot of _____ .

9 We like her way of singing. She has an interesting _____ .

10 During the movie, their _____ was terrible. They talked loudly and left early.

3 READING

Look at the questions in Reading Check Part A on page 102. Then read the story.

Mean Judges

1   A **contestant** sings a song on a **reality TV** show. The judges listen. One judge smiles. This judge is nice. She says kind things about the contestant's song. Another judge doesn't smile. He is mean. He says, "Your song is terrible!"

2   The contestant believes the mean judge. She likes him better. The other contestants also like him. Why do they all prefer the mean judge?

3   Mean people seem important. They seem like **experts**, and we believe them. We don't always believe nice people. A nice judge may lie to us. A mean judge tells the truth.

4   Simon Cowell is a famous mean judge on reality TV. Some of his shows are *Pop Idol*, *American Idol*, *X Factor*, and *Britain's Got Talent*. Simon is nasty. He doesn't like most of the contestants. If Simon likes someone, that person is very happy. They shout, "Simon likes me! Simon likes me!"

5   What about the TV **audience**? The audience also likes the mean judge! We don't like unpleasant people at work or school. So why are unpleasant judges on TV **popular**?

Professor Steven Reiss has an answer. Reiss studied reality 6
TV audiences. He asked 239 adults, "Why do you watch reality
TV?" The study showed something important: Reality **TV
viewers** like to have **status**. In other words, they like to be
better than other people. To the audience, TV contestants seem
famous and important. Sometimes a mean judge's **behavior**
hurts a contestant's feelings. Sometimes the contestants cry. The
audience enjoys it. Why? The TV viewer thinks, "That contestant
is famous because he is on TV. He did poorly. I'm better than
that person."

Today many countries have *Idol* shows. For example, there 7
is *Asian Idol* in six Asian countries, *Türkstar* in Turkey, *Star
Academy* in some Arabic-speaking countries, and *Ídolos Brasil* in
Latin America. These shows usually have a mean judge. Many
judges copy Simon Cowell's nasty **style**. Every week, millions of
people **tune in** and watch these unpleasant judges. And every
week, the contestants try to please these judges. It's very clear.
All over the world, people love mean judges!

4 READING CHECK

A Are these sentences true or false? Write *T* (true) or *F* (false).

1 _____ Contestants believe mean judges on TV.

2 _____ TV viewers are sad if a contestant cries.

3 _____ Audiences and contestants like mean judges.

B Circle the letter of the best answer.

1 Contestants listen to mean judges because _____ .
   a mean judges will say, "You are good"
   b mean judges are mean to everyone
   c mean judges seem like experts

2 Which sentence is *not* true about Simon Cowell?
   a He is not nice on the show.
   b He is on TV in Turkey and Latin America.
   c Other judges copy his style.

3 If Simon Cowell likes a contestant, the contestant feels _____ .
   a popular
   b happy
   c unpleasant

4 What did Steven Reiss do?
   a He studied reality TV audiences.
   b He was in a reality TV audience.
   c He sang on a reality TV show.

5 Which is true about reality TV audiences?
   a They do not like mean judges.
   b They are famous and important.
   c They like to have status.

6 Sometimes contestants cry. Why do TV viewers enjoy that?
   a They think, "We're better than the contestant."
   b They do not like the contestant.
   c They want to be contestants.

7 People in other countries _____ .
   a watch Simon Cowell
   b also like mean judges
   c do not watch reality TV shows

5 VOCABULARY CHECK

A Retell the story. Fill in the blanks with the correct words from the box.

| audience | behavior | contestant | expert | popular |
| reality TV | status | style | tune in | TV viewers |

1 Many people like to watch _____ shows, like
American Idol.

2 They _____ to their favorite contest on TV every week.

3 On the show, the _____ sings a song or dances.

4 Some judges are mean. Many people like these mean judges. They are
very _____ .

5 The singers believe a mean judge. He seems like a/an

_____ .

6 The _____ enjoys the show. They also like the mean judge.

7 We don't like people's bad _____ at work. But we like it
on TV.

8 Steven Reiss asked 239 _____ , "Why do you watch
reality TV?"

9 They like to have _____ . They want to be better than
the people on TV.

10 Simon Cowell is a famous judge with a nasty _____ .
Some other judges copy it.

B Make a word from the story. Put the letters in parentheses ( ) in the correct
order. Write the word in the sentence.

1 Each _____*contestant*_____ sings three songs in the contest. (tontecnats)

2 The _____ at the show was very big. There were 750
people there. (udaneeci)

3 If a TV show is boring, a TV _____ will usually change
the channel. (eewirv)

4 Science fiction movies are _____ . Millions of people
enjoy them. (laprupo)

5 People enjoy _____ TV shows all over the world. (lareyti)

6 APPLYING READING SKILLS

*Main ideas are the most important information in a reading. Supporting details tell you more about the main ideas. **Finding main ideas and supporting details** will help you understand a reading better.*

A Match the main ideas of the reading with the supporting details. Write the letter of each detail in the correct box.

MAIN IDEA	SUPPORTING DETAILS
1 Contestants like mean judges. ☐ ☐	**a** Mean judges seem like experts. **b** Reality TV viewers like to have status. **c** They think, "We're better than the unhappy contestants."
2 Audiences like mean judges. ☐ ☐	**d** Mean judges tell the truth.

B Find two supporting details for this main idea in the reading.

Reality TV shows with mean judges are popular all over the world.

a _____

b _____

7 DISCUSSION

Talk about these questions in pairs or groups.

1 What are some examples of reality TV programs in your country?
2 Are there mean judges on these shows? What do you think of them?
3 Should judges always say something nice to contestants? Explain your answer.

14

The Uncanny Valley

1 TOPIC PREVIEW

A Some robots look like humans. How are these robots different from humans? Put a check (✓) next to the most important differences. Share your answers with your classmates.

1 _____ a robot's eyes

2 _____ a robot's hands

3 _____ a robot's mouth

4 _____ a robot's voice

5 _____ a robot's walk

B Read the title of this chapter. Look at the picture. Then talk about these questions.

1 Were you ever afraid to watch a children's movie? Why or why not?
2 Look at the pictures. How do you feel about the robot? Explain your answer.
3 What do you think the reading will be about?

2 VOCABULARY PREVIEW

A Read the word lists. Which words do you know? Put a check (✓) next to them. Compare your answers with a partner. Then look up any new words in a dictionary.

TV and Film Studies	Academic Word List	Psychology
animated cartoon computer-generated filmmaker	positive response technology	anxious emotion scare (v.)

The chart shows some important words from the reading. These words are related to TV and film studies, psychology, and the Academic Word List (AWL). For more information about the AWL, see page 121.

B Fill in the blanks with words from Part A.

1 Love is a very strong _____ .

2 Big dogs often _____ small children.

3 Today we do a lot of our work with _____ , like computers and other electronic devices.

4 Many children love _____ movies with talking animals or flying cars.

5 The audience loved the movie. They had a very good _____ to it.

6 He's worried about the test today. He feels _____ .

7 A/An _____ makes movies.

8 Most artists don't use pencil and paper to make the people in video games. These characters are _____ .

9 Children always laugh at characters like Mickey Mouse in a funny _____ .

10 She always sees the good side of things. She is a very _____ person.

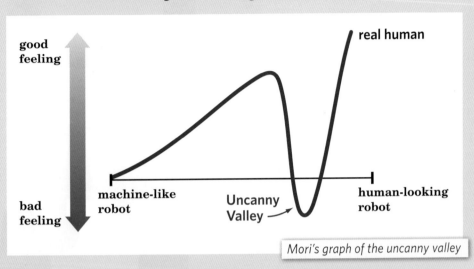

Look at the questions in Reading Check Part A on page 109. Then read the story.

The Uncanny Valley

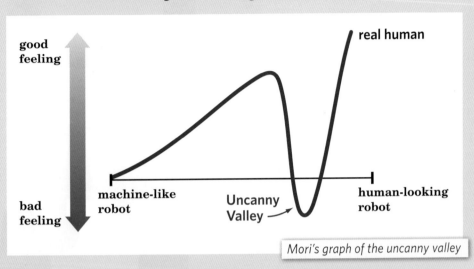

Mori's graph of the uncanny valley

One afternoon, six-year-old Emily Hamilton and her mother 1
saw the movie *The Polar Express*. It's an **animated** movie. The
story is from a popular book for children. A famous Hollywood
actor does one of the voices. It's a happy movie. The characters
look almost like real people.

But Emily and her mother didn't enjoy the movie. They felt 2
anxious, but they didn't know why. Something was strange
about the movie. Many people had the same feeling. They felt
uncomfortable. But why?

A man in Japan has the answer. For many years, Professor 3
Masahiro Mori studied people's feelings about robots. He learned
this: Some robots look like machines. We usually like this type
of robot. Other robots look a little like humans. We like this
type of robot even more. But sometimes robots look a lot like
humans. Suddenly our feelings change. We do not like these
human-looking robots at all!

Mori has a name for the change in our **emotions**. He calls it 4
the "uncanny[1] valley.[2]" In the uncanny valley, the robots look

---

[1] *uncanny:* strange
[2] *valley:* an area of low land between hills or mountains

a lot like humans. They seem familiar but strange. We have a bad **response** to them. We feel uncomfortable.

5   Mori's ideas are true for movie characters, too. Most animated characters are lovable. Audiences like characters such as Shrek and Wall-E.[3] These characters aren't human, but we have a **positive** feeling about them. We also like the Simpsons[4] family. They are human characters, but they are **cartoons**. They don't look like real people. They make us relax and laugh. We feel good.

Wall-E

6   Many movie animators use computers. They make **computer-generated (CG)** characters. CG humans look almost like real people. But movie audiences don't like them. Something seems wrong. The CG humans move in the wrong way. Their skin looks strange. Most important, the eyes don't look alive. CG humans seem dead.

7   When do we start to feel uncomfortable? If characters look 90 percent like us, we feel OK. If characters look 95 percent like us, it seems strange.

8   This information is important for **filmmakers**. They tested the movie *Shrek* with children. The Princess Fiona character **scared** them. Why? She looked too much like a real person. So the animators made a new Princess Fiona. Now she is a cartoon, and she doesn't frighten anybody.

9   With new **technology**, animators can make very real-looking human characters. But they learned from *The Polar Express* and Princess Fiona. They don't want to scare their audience. They do not want to enter the uncanny valley.

---

[3] *Shrek and Wall-E:* two characters from animated movies
[4] *the Simpsons:* a cartoon family on a popular American TV program

4 READING CHECK

A Circle the letter of the best answer.

1 Masahiro Mori studied _____ .
 a people's feelings about robots
 b movie characters
 c animated movies

2 In the uncanny valley, _____ .
 a robots don't look like people
 b we relax and laugh
 c our feelings change suddenly

3 Which robots do we like best?
 a Robots that don't look like humans.
 b Robots that look a little like humans.
 c Robots that look a lot like humans.

B Are these sentences true or false? Write *T* (true) or *F* (false).

1 _____ *The Polar Express* is a happy movie, but many people didn't like it.

2 _____ Masahiro Mori makes robots.

3 _____ We usually like machine robots.

4 _____ People often have positive feelings about cartoons.

5 _____ We feel uncomfortable if computer-generated characters are 95 percent like us.

6 _____ CG humans move like real people.

7 _____ We have a bad response to the eyes of CG characters.

8 _____ Mori's studies are important for filmmakers.

9 _____ Animators changed Princess Fiona because she scared children.

10 _____ Filmmakers want very real-looking human CG characters in their movies.

5 VOCABULARY CHECK

A Retell the story. Fill in the blanks with the correct words from the box.

animated	anxious	cartoons	computer-generated	emotions
filmmakers	positive	response	scare	technology

1 *The Polar Express* is a/an _____ movie.

2 Some people didn't enjoy the movie. They felt _____ .

3 This is the reason: We like machine robots. But we see human-looking robots, and our _____ change. We don't like these robots.

4 This information is important for _____ . They don't want real-looking human characters in their animated movies.

5 In movies, sometimes _____ humans have strange eyes or skin. We don't enjoy these characters.

6 Animators can make funny _____ , such as Shrek. We like them.

7 We have a/an _____ feeling about those characters.

8 Today animators often use new _____ to make very real-looking human characters.

9 Some real-looking human characters _____ children. Filmmakers don't use them in movies.

10 Filmmakers want a good _____ to their movies.

B Find these words in the reading. Then for each word, find another word with a similar meaning. Write it on the lines.

1 anxious (par. 2)   _ _ _ _ _ _ _ _ _ _ _ _ _ (par. 2)

2 emotions (par. 4)   _ _ _ _ _ _ _ _ (par. 3)

3 positive (par. 5)   _ _ _ _ (par. 5)

4 scare (par. 8)   _ _ _ _ _ _ _ _ (par. 8)

6 APPLYING READING SKILLS

In a reading, you will often find answers to these questions: What is the cause, or why does something happen? What is the effect, or what is the result? **Finding causes and effects** *in a reading will help you understand it better.*

A Draw an arrow (→) from each cause to its effect

CAUSE	EFFECT
1 CG characters look 95 percent like us.	**a** People relax and laugh at them.
2 Animators use new technology.	**b** The audience feels anxious.
3 Cartoons don't look like real people.	**c** They can make very real-looking human characters.

B Practice finding causes and effects. Look back at the reading, and find one effect for each cause in the chart.

CAUSE	EFFECT
1 Sometimes a robot looks a lot like a human.	_____
2 The eyes of CG characters don't look alive.	_____
3 The first Princess Fiona scared children.	_____

7 DISCUSSION

Talk about these questions in pairs or groups.

1 Do computer-generated characters in movies ever scare you? If so, which ones?

2 Name a favorite animated character. Why do you like that character?

3 Many adults enjoy animated movies. Why is this true?

CHAPTER
15
A New Language

1 TOPIC PREVIEW

A Learning a new language is not easy. Which parts are difficult for you? Put a check (✓) next to them. Then add your own idea. Share your answers with your classmates.

_____ listening

_____ speaking

_____ spelling

_____ vocabulary

_____ writing

_____ _____ (your idea)

B Read the title of this chapter. Look at the picture. Then talk about these questions.

1 Do you like movies in a foreign language? Why or why not?
2 Look at the picture. Do you think these characters speak English? Why or why not?
3 What do you think the reading will be about?

2 VOCABULARY PREVIEW

A Read the word lists. Which words do you know? Put a check (✓) next to them. Compare your answers with a partner. Then look up any new words in a dictionary.

TV and Film Studies	Academic Word List	Language Studies
(film) **crew** **director** **set** (*n.*)	**create** **project** (*n.*)	**consonant** **grammar** **pronunciation** **translate** **vowel**

The chart shows some important words from the reading. These words are related to TV and film studies, language studies, and the Academic Word List (AWL). For more information about the AWL, see page 121.

B Write the word from Part A next to its definition.

1 The rules of a language. They help you make sentences:

_____

2 People make movies here: _____

3 Make something new: _____

4 We work for a long time on this activity at school or work:

_____

5 This group of people works on a movie: _____

6 Change words into a different language: _____

7 Examples of this type of sound are *a, e, i, o,* and *u*:

_____

8 Examples of this type of sound are *b, j, r,* and *m*: _____

9 This person is in charge of the actors. He or she helps them with their parts: _____

10 How we say the sounds of a language: _____

Look at the questions in Reading Check Part A on page 116. Then read the story.

A New Language

1   Did anyone ever greet you like this?: "Kaltxì. Ngaru lu fpom srak?" Probably not. These words mean "Hello. Are you well?" in Na'vi. Na'vi is a new, man-made language. There are already over 5,000 languages in the world. Why did someone want to **create** a completely new language?

2   The story begins with the movie, *Avatar*. James Cameron was the **director**. For this movie, Cameron invented a world called Pandora. Artists created beautiful plants and amazing animals for Pandora. They also created nine-foot tall blue aliens.[1] They were the Na'vi people. Cameron wanted one more thing: a special language for the Na'vi.

3   Cameron started to work on the language. He created about 30 words. But it wasn't enough. He needed help with the **project**, so he asked Paul Frommer. Frommer is a professor at the University of Southern California. He studies languages. Frommer liked the idea, so he took the job.

---

[1] *aliens:* living things from another planet, not Earth

Frommer studied Cameron's words. First, he thought about the sounds. He chose 20 **consonants** and 7 **vowels**. These are sounds in English, too. Na'vi also has special sounds like *tx* and *ng*. Next, he created rules of **grammar**. For example, in Na'vi, the word order is not important. Finally, he created a vocabulary of about 1,000 words. He finished the project in six months.

4

Then Frommer worked on the movie **set**. He taught Na'vi to the actors. They had special language classes. Frommer also recorded the Na'vi language. The actors listened to it on their iPods. He **translated** four songs from English to Na'vi, too. He helped the singers with the **pronunciation**. Sometimes Cameron needed a new word. Then Frommer created one. Soon the film **crew** started to speak in Na'vi. Sometimes someone made a mistake. Then other people laughed and said, "Skxawng!" This means "stupid person."

5

Today many people are learning Na'vi. There are Na'vi Web sites, dictionaries, and fan groups. The fans create new words, and the language grows. This makes Frommer very happy. The Na'vi language now has a life of its own.

6

4 READING CHECK

A Match the people to the actions.

1 James Cameron ____   **a** created the Na'vi language

2 Paul Frommer ____   **b** directed the movie *Avatar*

3 actors in *Avatar* ____   **c** learned to speak Na'vi for the movie

B Circle the letter of the best answer.

1 Na'vi is a ____ language.
   a man-made
   b very old
   c large

2 James Cameron hired Paul Frommer to ____.
   a write the Na'vi language
   b be an actor in his movie
   c be a professor

3 How many Na'vi words did Frommer create?
   a about 30
   b about 20
   c about 1,000

4 What did Frommer do first?
   a He wrote rules for Na'vi grammar.
   b He chose the sounds of Na'vi.
   c He taught Na'vi to the actors.

5 What is *not* important in the Na'vi language?
   a sounds
   b the number of words
   c word order

6 Who did *not* create new Na'vi words?
   a Paul Frommer
   b fans
   c the film crew

7 Which sentence is *not* true?
   a Frommer wrote songs in English for the movie.
   b Sometimes the film crew used Na'vi words.
   c Frommer taught Na'vi language classes.

5 VOCABULARY CHECK

A Retell the story. Fill in the blanks with the correct words from the box.

consonants	create	crew	director	grammar
project	pronunciation	set	translated	vowels

1 James Cameron was the _____ of the movie *Avatar*.

2 Cameron wanted a special language for the Na'vi in his movie. He hired Paul Frommer for this _____.

3 First, Frommer chose the sounds for Na'vi. He chose 20 _____.

4 He chose 7 _____.

5 Then he wrote rules for the _____ of Na'vi. The word order isn't important.

6 He worked together with Cameron and the actors on the movie _____.

7 The film _____ sometimes used Na'vi words, too, like *skxawng*.

8 Frommer also _____ songs into Na'vi.

9 Then he helped the singers with the _____ of Na'vi.

10 Today many people are learning Na'vi. Fans _____ new Na'vi words every day. It is a growing language.

B Which word does *not* belong in each row? Cross it out.

1 grammar   pronunciation   vocabulary   project

2 actor   movie set   director   film crew

3 invent   create   make   translate

4 Na'vi   English   Pandora   Avatar

5 word order   consonant   vowel   sound

6 APPLYING READING SKILLS

*How many words do you read in a minute? That is your reading speed. You can practice **reading faster**. Then your reading speed will go up, and reading for your classes will be easier.*

A Reread "A New Language" on pages 114–115, and time yourself. Write this information: your starting time, your finishing time, and the number of minutes in between. Then calculate your reading speed.

> **Story title:** "A New Language" (341 words)
> Starting time: _____
> Finishing time: _____
> Total reading time: _____ minutes
> *Reading speed: _____ words per minute

*To calculate your reading speed, divide the number of words in the reading (341 words) by your total reading time. (How many minutes did you need to finish the reading?)

B Now reread "Mean Judges" (347 words) on pages 100–101 or "The Uncanny Valley" (441 words) on pages 107–108. Time yourself. Write the title of the story and your times below. Then calculate your reading speed.

> **Story title:** _____ (_____ words)
> Starting time: _____
> Finishing time: _____
> Total reading time: _____ minutes
> Reading speed: _____ words per minute

7 DISCUSSION

Talk about these questions in pairs or groups.

1 Why did James Cameron create a new language for *Avatar*?
2 Why do some fans enjoy man-made languages like Na'vi? Do you?
3 Create three words for a new language. What do the words mean? What is the pronunciation of the words? Was it difficult to create new words?

VOCABULARY REVIEW

Chapter **13**	Chapter **14**	Chapter **15**
TV and Film Studies	**TV and Film Studies**	**TV and Film Studies**
audience · contestant · reality TV · tune in · TV viewer	animated · cartoon · computer-generated · filmmaker	(film) **crew** · **director** · **set**
Academic Word List	**Academic Word List**	**Academic Word List**
expert · status · style	positive · technology	create · project (n.)
Sociology	**Psychology**	**Language Studies**
behavior · popular	anxious · emotion · response · scare (v.)	consonant · grammar · pronunciation · translate · vowel

Find words in the chart above that match the definitions. Answers to 1–4 are from Chapter 13. Answers to 5–8 are from Chapter 12. Answers to 9–12 are from Chapter 15.

1 This person knows a lot about something: _____

2 This group of people watches a movie or TV show: _____

3 How a person acts and says things: _____

4 To turn on the TV to watch a show: _____

5 Happy about your life and your future: _____

6 To make someone afraid: _____

7 Worried about something: _____

8 A funny drawing of a person or animal: _____

9 A place to make a movie: _____

10 To invent something or make something new: _____

11 To change a word from one language to another language:

_____

12 A school or work activity. It has a goal and takes a long time:

_____

VOCABULARY IN USE

Work with a partner or small group. Talk about the questions below.

1 Which **reality TV** shows do you enjoy? Why do you like them?

2 Do you like to **create** things? If so, what do you like to create? If not, why not?

3 What **technology** is most important to you? Can you live without it? Why or why not?

4 What subjects are you an **expert** in?

5 What movies are **popular** right now? Which ones do you like?

6 Do any animals **scare** you? If so, which ones?

7 Who is your favorite movie **director**? Why do you like his or her movies?

8 What types of class **projects** do you enjoy? Explain your answer.

INTERVIEW

Interview another student. Take turns asking and answering these questions.

1 Which story is the most interesting to you? Why?

2 Think about "Mean Judges" and imagine this: You are a reality TV contestant. How do you feel? What are the judges like? Which judge do you like best? Why?

3 Think about "A New Language" and imagine this: You are an actor in *Avatar*. What part of the job do you like best? Why?

WRITING

Write about one of these people.

- Steven Reiss
- Masahiro Mori
- Paul Frommer

In your writing, answer these questions. Write three or four sentences in a paragraph.

- Who is the person?
- What is his job?
- What did he do?

WEBQUEST

Find more information about the topics in this unit. Go to www.cambridge.org/readthis and follow the instructions for doing a WebQuest. Search for facts. Have fun. Good luck!

The Academic Word List

What are the most common words in academic English? Which words appear most frequently in readings in different academic subject areas? Dr. Averil Coxhead, who is currently a Senior Lecturer at Victoria University of Wellington in New Zealand, did research to try to answer these questions. The result was the Academic Word List (AWL).

Coxhead studied readings in English from many different academic fields. She found 570 words or word families that appear in many of those readings. These are words like *estimate* and *estimation*; *analyze*, *analysis*, and *analytical*; *evident*, *evidence*, and *evidently* – words that you can expect to find when reading a sociology text, a computer science text, or even a music studies text. So if you want to read nonfiction in English or academic English, these are the words that are going to be most useful for you to study and learn.

When you study the readings in *Read This!*, you will study words that belong to two different academic subject areas. These words will help you understand the topic of each reading. In addition, you will study AWL words in the readings. Learning the AWL words will help you, not just when you are reading on that topic, but also when you read any academic text, because these words are likely to come up in your reading again and again.

In the following list, we show you all the words that are from the Academic Word List that are in all four books of the *Read This!* series. Many of these words appear in several of the readings. However, the words in the list that are followed by letters and numbers are words that are the focus of study in one of the readings. The letters and numbers show which book and chapter the word appears in. For example, "access RT2, 13" tells you that you study the word *access* in *Read This!* Book 2, Chapter 13. When the letters and numbers after the word appear in color, that tells you that the word is the focus of study in this *Read This!* book.

From time to time you might want to study the words in this list and test yourself. By going to the chapter where the word appears, you can see the words in context, which is one of the best ways to study new or unfamiliar words.

The following list shows the AWL words that appear in the *Read This!* series.

A

academy

access RT2, 13

accurate

accurately RT2, 6

achieve

achievement RT1, 5

adjust RT3, 14

administration RTI, 3

administrator RTI, 1

adult RTI, 1; RT2, 12

affect RTI, 8; RT3, 11

alternative

analysis RT2, 12; RT3, 13

analyze

appreciate RT3, 1

approach RT3, 1

approaching

approximately RT1, 13

area RTI, 12; RT1, 3

assist RTI, 5; RT2, 5

assistance

authority RT2, 13

available

aware

awareness RTI, 10; RT3, 8

B

beneficial

benefit RT2, 9

C

challenge RT1, 7; RT2, 2;
    RT3, 3

challenged

challenging RT2, 14

channel

chapter

chemical RT3, 5

civil

classical

coincidence RT1, 9

collapse RT2, 13

comment

commit

communicate RT1, 1

communication

compensation

complex RT3, 4

computer

concentrate RT3, 14

concentration RT2, 14

conduct

conflict RT3, 10

constant

construct RT3, 1

construction

consultant

consume RT2, 9

contact RT3, 4

contrast

contribute

contribution RT1, 7

controversial RT3, 11

conventional RT3, 7

couple

create RTI, 15; RT1, 3

creative RT2, 4

crucial RT2, 15

cultural

culture

cycle RT3, 6

D

data RT2, 9

define

design RTI, 4; RT1, 14; RT3, 3

designer

detect RT2, 6

device RTI, 7; RT3, 9

discriminate

discrimination

display RT3, 10

disposable RT3, 5

distinct RT3, 2

distinction

distinctive

distinctly

diverse RT3, 2

document RT3, 10

documented

domain

E

energy RT1, 15

enormous RT1, 10

environment

environmental

environmentally

equipment RTI, 11; RT3, 8

establish RT3, 6

estate

estimate RT2, 13

eventually

evidence RT2, 12; RT3, 12

evolve RT3, 15

exhibit RT3, 11

expand RT2, 7

expert RTI, 13; RT1, 2; RT2, 10; RT3, 5

export RT1, 12

F

feature RT1, 8

federal

federations

fee

file RTI, 2; RT1, 5

final

finally RTI, 7

flexibility RT3, 9

flexible

focus RTI, 2; RT1, 6

foundation RT3, 3

function RT1, 8

G

generated

generation RT2, 13; RT3, 15

global RT1, 10

goal RTI, 10; RT3, 8

grade RTI, 1

guideline RT1, 8

H

highlight

I

identical RT2, 11

identification RT3, 13

identified

identify RT2, 6

identifying

identity RT2, 10

illegal RT3, 12

image RT2, 4

impact RT2, 15

individual RT3, 7

injure

injured

injury RT3, 9

institute RT2, 4

instructions

intelligence

intelligent

intense RT3, 6

interact RTI, 3

interaction RT3, 2

interactive

investigate RT2, 11; RT3, 12

investigating

investigation

investigative

investigator

investor

involve

isolate RT2, 8

issue

item

J

job

L

layer RT3, 3

legal

liberate RT3, 11

locate

location RTI, 11

M

maintain RT2, 5

major

maximum RT3, 14

media RTI, 6

medical

mental RTI, 9; RT2, 14; RT3, 8

method RT2, 2

military

monitor RT3, 4

N

network RT1, 5

normal RTI, 8; RT2, 3

normally RT1, 1

O

obviously RT2, 10

occur RT2, 8

odd RTI, 4

option RT2, 15

P

participate RT1, 4

participation RT3, 7

partner RT1, 2

percent

period RTI, 8

philosophy

physical RT2, 8; RT3, 8

physically

policy RT3, 10

positive RTI, 14

predict RT1, 11; RT2, 6; RT3, 1

prime

principle RT3, 10

procedure RT2, 3

process RT2, 9; RT3, 5

project RTI, 15; RT1, 5; RT3, 3

promote

psychological

psychologist

psychology

publish RT3, 12

publisher RT1, 4

publishing

purchase

R

range

ratio RT1, 8

reaction RTI, 6; RT3, 11

recover RT2, 3

recovered

recovery RT3, 9

region RT3, 5

register RT1, 11

registration

relax RTI, 2

relaxing

release RT3, 4

reluctant RT3, 2

rely

remove

require RT3, 13

research RT1, 1

researcher RTI, 9; RT2, 1

resource

respond RT1, 7; RT2, 8

response RTI, 14

restrict RT2, 9

restricted

restricting

restriction

reveal RT3, 5

role RT2, 13

route RT3, 14

S

section

security RT1, 2

sequence RT1, 9

shift RT3, 15

significant RT3, 2

significantly RT2, 9

similar RT2, 1

similarity RT1, 9

site RT2, 6

source RT1, 15; RT2, 7; RT3, 12

specific RT1, 14

specifically RT3, 9

specification

specify

stability RT3, 10

stabilize

stable

status RTI, 13

strategy RT1, 12

stress RTI, 2; RT2, 14

stressed

structure RT1, 13; RT2, 4; RT3, 3

style RTI, 13; RT1, 4; RT3, 15

survey RT3, 4

survive RTI, 7; RT2, 3; RT3, 6

survivor

sustainable

symbol RT1, 3; RT2, 7; RT3, 11

T

tape RT1, 6

target RTI, 10

task

team

technology RTI, 14

theory RT2, 2

trace

tradition

traditional RT3, 2

traditionally RTI, 5

transit

transition RT3, 15

transport RT2, 5; RT3, 13

U

uniform

unique RTI, 11; RT1, 14; RT2, 11; RT3, 1

V

vehicle RT3, 13

virtual

visual RTI, 9

volunteer RT1, 15

Art Credits